CW00735634

LIVERPOOL
Born and Bred

by Peter Kelly

ACKNOWLEDGEMENTS

To my wife Else for the million cups of tea while my head was in the PC.

To my brother Chris for the help and guidance through the mysteries of writing.

In addition, all my family and the people I met who helped make my life so interesting.

Thanks to Dewi Williams in Canada for his kind permission to reproduce the photographs of the Liverpool Overhead railway.

Thanks to Ron the Tram for his pictures.

And thanks to anyone else whose photographs I have used only after exhaustive searches for the owner of any material I found on the public domain of the Internet.

First Published 2009 by Appin Press, an inprint of Countyvise Limited.
14 Appin Road, Birkenhead, Wirral CH41 9HH.

Copyright © 2009 Peter Kelly

The right of Peter Kelly to be identified as the author of this work has been asserted by him in accordance with the Copyright, Design and Patents Act 1988.

British Library Cataloguing in Publication Data.
A catalogue record for this book is available from the British Library.

ISBN 978 1 906205 30 0

All rights reserved. No part of this publication may be reproduced, stored in a retrieval system, or transmitted, in any other form, or by any other means, electronic, chemical, mechanic, photocopying, recording or otherwise, without the prior permission of the publisher.

PROLOGUE

Suddenly, there was a horrible scream from behind - "You Little Bastard". I swung around and there to my horror was a big angry soldier running towards me. I was off like a shot across the park but the pursuer was gaining on me. His legs were much longer than mine were and I could hear his hobnailed boots as they crashed into the earth, coming closer and closer. I was in a terrible state of panic. What is he going to do to me? My heart was racing faster than my legs; I could sense him right behind me. I will never know to this day why I suddenly stopped and curled up into a ball but it did the trick. He went flying right over the top of me and crashed in an untidy heap about three yards in front. I sprang up, dodged past his sprawled out body and escaped out of the park, blending into the throng of shoppers. Behind me in the distance, I could hear loud laughter and cries of 'Ya soft shite, you couldn't even catch a kid' coming from his colleagues.

I avoided the park route after that fright and resumed to taking the longer one down Jubilee Drive. This was a very monotonous walk home for a small boy, with nothing to stimulate the mind. I was happy when one day, some schoolmates introduced me to the art of 'Legging'.

Author aged 19 in Malaya

First Casualty

The first memory I can recall must have been two years after I was born. I was playing on a rug in front of a warm fire. Someone big, probably my father was sitting in an armchair reading a newspaper. My attention was on a small yellow bird; I could hear the noise from its feet as it walked around the linoleum floor covering just off the edge of the rug. The little creature seemed to know I couldn't move quickly and was strutting around, displaying a cocky attitude. I remember wanting to get nearer, to get my hands on it, to me it was a toy just like other toys I had played with, but somehow, this one was different. Every time I moved forward, the toy would walk further away, just keeping out of reach. My happiness was draining away and being replaced by a new feeling, which I didn't like. Suddenly, the door from the hallway opened and the toy disappeared through the tiny gap under the door. It did a sort of roll onto its side, its body flattened out; the tip of its upturned wing was the last I saw as it vanished from sight. Its lifeless remains were probably thrown into the dustbin or even flushed away down the toilet. People had no time to be sentimental about pets, a war was looming and times were to get a lot harder.

I was born into a loving and hard working Catholic family in Liverpool on a cold February day in 1938. My parents lived by the Catholic code of abstaining from birth prevention; consequently my mother had ten pregnancies. I am the fourth of six surviving children.

My Mother's Dad, William Grant (my grandfather) was of highland stock. His father, John, had sailed down from Loth in Sutherlandshire Scotland on a Tea Clipper in the 1860s. His voyage ended at Chester, which was a busy port at the time.

That beautiful old City on the river Dee soon lost its merchant trade when the Iron ships took over from sail. Their draft was too deep for the shallow waters around Chester and it wasn't long before the whole of the Dee in that area silted up. John Grant had been trading as a Tea Merchant in Scotland and he continued in that trade in Cheshire in addition to dealing in Lime, a comparatively new product that was mixed with Portland cement for the building trade. He eventually settled in Wrexham, North Wales where he married Jane Humphreys, a fine seamstress. Jane opened a dress shop in Bank Street where they both lived in the upstairs rooms. Sometime later, William Grant became the agent for the local Liberal Party Candidate in Wrexham.

My Father's Dad, John Kelly, came from Dundalk in Ireland. He was a merchant seaman who sailed all through the First World War on the SS *Sotero*, steaming out of Liverpool to Genoa in Italy and Bilbao in Northern Spain. After the war, John Kelly settled in St. Helen's Lancashire. He became a foreman at Pilkingtons Glassworks and was introduced to King Edward

Theresa Kelly, front left, carrying glass

V11 and Queen Alexandra when they made a royal visit to St. Helens in the early 1900s. One of granddad's younger daughters, Theresa, worked at Pilkingtons as a plate glass carrier. At the age of fifteen, she worked a sixty-hour week, which was quite normal. (See photograph on previous page). John Kelly (my paternal grandfather) married a beautiful Lancashire Rose, Mary Agnes Todd. They had thirteen children, my father being the fourth eldest. Dad told us a story of how, during the First World War, he would be sent to find the newspaper vendor for the final edition of the *Liverpool Echo*. His mother wanted to see what ships had been sunk by the German U-boats.

(1917 Feb. 1 - Germany began unrestricted submarine warfare. German subs sank 500 ships in the first two months, over 1,000,000 tons. The bigger U-boats carried sixteen torpedoes versus the earlier six.)

If the SS *Sotero* was not listed in the Stop Press, (a blank portion on the back page reserved for late news) the family could breathe a sigh of relief and sleep soundly for one more night.

Gladstone Dock

Sometimes we only saw Dad at weekends; he worked all the hours he could to support his family. We were in bed by the time he got home and he was up early and away the next morning before we were awake. Mother was always busy with washing, cooking, sewing, knitting, shopping or breastfeeding; the list seemed endless. She was a small woman without an ounce of extra fat on her body and without an extra shilling to spend on herself, yet she had to find that shilling every week to put into the hand of the parish priest when he called. Dad on the other hand was a big man, heavily built with powerful arms and big hands. He was a warm, loving man who cared passionately about his family and if necessary, would protect them with his life.

It was some time later when I learned that Dad had several cage birds and the little yellow one that had come to the end of its life was his favourite Canary. These were the days before mass consumer goods; people amused themselves with either reading, using their hands to create things or among others, keeping small pets that didn't cost a lot of money in food.

Dad started work as a Docker during the First World War when he was just seventeen years of age, that's when women worked there. The docks were a very dangerous place to work. People were injured on a daily basis and spent their days constantly in peril as no health and safety procedures had been set in place. Some men died and some caught terrible diseases that were brought in by ships' crews from far-flung lands. My Dad has worked on ships that had smallpox; he was very lucky not to catch that very contagious disease or we could all have suffered. It was survival of the fittest in those days. Dockworkers did not have permanent employment; there was no holiday pay, no unemployment benefit, nobody had rights. They had to report early in the morning on the quayside of a ship that had just berthed up, and hope they would be picked for a day's work. The Ganger or Tallyman would choose only those men who he knew, would give him a good day's work. He would put a metal talley disc into their hands and at the end of the day; they would swap their tally for a day's pay. Dad was a hard worker; he was very well known and thought highly of by all his workmates. In his mid twenties, he was trained as a crane driver at Gladstone Dock, the first big dock on the Mersey that ships' crews saw, as they sailed in from ports all over the world.

His crane was one of several giant machines mounted on the roofs of enormous quayside warehouses, where the goods, lifted out of the ships, were stored before being transported to the four corners of Britain by road, rail or barge.

During the Second World War, Dad worked long hours loading and unloading essential supplies for the war effort. He witnessed several enemy-bombing raids on ships berthed along the seven miles of Liverpool docks, from his position high up in his crane cab. He told us how he could see wave after wave of German planes coming in over Bidston Hill Observatory on the Wirral, the navigators using the observatory as a landmark as they headed directly for the docks. It was said that Hitler wanted to destroy the dock system to stop supplies coming in from America. Dockworkers would run for their lives when the attacks started and had to get back to work as soon as the all-clear siren was heard. During these raids, Dad was always worried about what was happening at home, he would only find out after his shift was finished.

The seven nights of the 1941 May Blitz (1st-7th May) were the heaviest consecutive nights of bombing experienced by Liverpool people during the whole of the Second World War. In those few nights, around six hundred and eighty planes dropped eight hundred and seventy tonnes of high explosives and over 112,000 incendiaries (firebombs) on the area, killing more than seventeen hundred people and making around seventy six thousand homeless. It was thought that Hitler was trying to wipe Liverpool off the face of the map.

On the worst night of the Blitz, 3 May 1941, the SS *Malakand*, a steamer loaded with over 1000 tons of shells and bombs, was destroyed in Huskisson No 2 dock. It is thought a deflated barrage balloon fell onto her deck and burst into flames. As it burnt and with all the light it provided, German bombs targeted and set fire to neighbouring sheds and soon the *Malakand* itself was ablaze. Despite all attempts to put out the fire, she had to be abandoned. The resulting catastrophic explosion completely destroyed the dock. Parts of the ship were thrown up to two and a half miles away. Miraculously, considering the size of the blast, only four people were killed.

Dad was in his crane at the beginning of that raid and as the *Malakand* caught fire, the whole of the Seaforth dock area was evacuated.

During the war, no one was allowed to show any light from their windows or elsewhere as this could give the German bombers an indication of their intended targets. The 'Black-out' made the whole city an eerie place during the hours of darkness and due to there being no trams running, Dad had to walk the seven miles home many times.

The Ghost

Our dad was always one for telling good stories and we never knew whether they were truth or fiction. One night around the dinner table, he told us all about the previous night's walk home, when he met a man who was going his way in the dark. They had a short conversation about the terrible bombing raids that had been going on every night for the past week. They were walking past many bombed out ruins of houses and works premises when the stranger said "Good night". Dad replied and turned around to see where the man was going. The figure walked up three stone steps that had been the front entrance to a house and which was now just a complete ruin, with roof beams tottering at precarious angles and plaster covered brickwork laying in heaps. Dad saw the figure fade and disappear into the darkness at the top of the steps. His hair bristled on the back of his neck as he turned and quickened his pace for home. It was only then, when he realised he had not heard any footsteps from the stranger as he walked beside him. I don't know about the rest of the family but the hair stood up on the back of my head as he finished his story.

I loved listening to stories being told by grown-ups. To me, they were very special times and something that is sadly missing in today's culture.

Raining Bombs

During one of the bombing raids when Dad was at work, mother tucked us up into the make shift shelter that had been put together in the living room. A big spring bed with iron frame had been brought downstairs and placed across, between the sideboard and dining table. Another mattress was put on top and we slept underneath in our 'Den', which we called the 'Blue Room' because a great big blue Eiderdown was draped down on all sides. Each night before bedtime, we kids spent an hour playing war games, climbing in, out and on top before finally tiring ourselves out and snuggling up in the new shelter. Hours later, we could sense Mam with baby Terence, crawling into our den in the dark and pulling the blankets over us. I woke up and could hear her muttering in a low voice "I hope Dad's alright at work" before settling down herself. Dad was down at the docks, working the night shift.

Our sister, Monica, and brother Gerald had been evacuated to North Wales. Bryan, another elder brother should have gone with them but he whinged so much that Mam had to keep him home. I was too young to be evacuated. Another sister, Patricia had died from pneumonia when she was just a tiny baby.

The sound of sirens woke us up, followed by a heavy droning, getting louder and louder, we could hear distant explosions.

Kids in Street

"Oh my God, they're bombing the docks again," said Mam. She started comforting us as the droning sounds began vibrating the cups and saucers in the kitchen. I could hear Bryan saying, "Are they going to drop a bomb on us Mam?" "Shush son, Shush, go to sleep" she replied. She couldn't bring herself to tell a little white lie because she knew, that any minute, a bomb could drop on us and that would be the end, at least we would all have gone together. What if it had happened? Poor Dad would have lost our Mam and three of his children. The German planes were passing right overhead; it sounded as though there were hundreds of them. The explosions were getting nearer and bombs started dropping all around the area. I put my hands over my ears and closed my eyes as tight as I could, hoping it would all go away. Suddenly, there was a huge explosion close by, the single light bulb went out, and a lot of soot fell down the chimney, making it hard to breath. We could hear screams from women and girls somewhere outside. Eventually the bombers passed over and their noise faded into the distance. The anti-aircraft guns in Kensington Gardens had stopped firing and things were quietening down. Somebody with a heavy footstep was running down the street and the sound of fire engine bells could be heard all over the city. Then the one sound that everybody was waiting for, the 'All clear' sirens. The Germans had finished their bombing raid and had gone home, for this night at least.

We settled down to get some sleep but I don't think Mam slept a bit that night, I heard her in the back kitchen making herself a cup of tea. The one thing that people went for whenever there was a crisis was a cup of tea. The therapeutic comfort from holding your hands around a warm cup of tea after any shock to the system is extremely satisfying.

In the morning, we couldn't get out through the front door, it seemed to be jammed. We went out through the yard and along the entry to see what damage had been done in the street. I was holding on to my mother's hand as we stood on the edge of a massive hole in the middle of the street, water was pouring out of broken pipes at the bottom of the crater, slowly filling it up. The neighbours' houses on both side of the street nearest the crater had been blown to smithereens. It was strange being able to look at the wallpaper on what was left of their bedroom walls. I felt Mam's hand tighten and heard her cry of shock as we turned to look at the front of our house, Like all the others, it didn't have one pane of glass left in the windows and lots of slates were missing off the roof. Someone helped Mam to open our front door from the outside; we went indoors to have a look at the front room. I heard her saying something about her curtains being shredded to pieces as we stood in the parlour surveying the damage. My attention was on the many pieces of sharp glass, which were embedded in the plaster on the walls, both tyres of Dad's bike had been punctured by the same glass but that didn't matter, the chain had been broken for weeks. There was also glass embedded in the woodwork of the old second hand piano standing in the corner, the previous tenant had left it there.

"That brown paper your Dad stuck on the windows didn't do much good," she said. The authorities had advised everyone to stick brown paper strips on their windowpanes to stop such a thing happening.

Hiding in terror

One afternoon, I was watching our Milkman, Ernie Bradbury; he had some cows in a yard and stables at the top of the street. His mother ran a little dairy shop next door to the yard where she sold a variety of dairy products and fizzy pop. On the shelves were bottles of Sarsaparilla, Dandelion and Burdock, and my favourite, Cream Soda. The stoppers were made of porcelain with a red rubber washer around the neck and a strong metal sprung catch which you had to use your two thumbs to click open, All bottles and glass food jars would have a deposit charged on them to ensure they were returned for re-use but they had to be clean or you wouldn't get your penny back for a one pound jam jar or tuppence for a two pound one. A few years later, on Saturday mornings, I would knock on four or five neighbours' doors, asking if they had any jamjars. I would nearly always get enough jars to make my entrance fee for the Kensington Picture house Saturday matinee that cost six pence. I never found out why but someone called the shop, 'Mrs Mac's Muck Shop' and it stuck. Above our heads, on the ceiling was a big coloured poster of a Bull's head with a ring through its nose and the giant letters, OXO. I often came out of the shop with a crick in my neck from staring upwards. I loved to go into the little urban farm next door where I experienced the sights, sounds and smells of the countryside in the middle of the city. Ernie was sitting on a small three-legged stool, milking a cow, I was watching the jets of milk hitting the insides of the bucket and listening to the ringing sounds the milk was making. I was transfixed, almost hypnotised by the steady movement of his hands, changing over from one teat to another. Two cats appeared and sat patiently by, waiting for their daily drop of milk. I was about three and a half years old at the time. Mother was having a cup of tea at Auntie Maude's who lived two doors away from the dairy. She wasn't a real Auntie; we called most women by those names who were family friends. Mother knew I would be safe playing outside. There was no fear of child molesters in my young days. Traffic was very sparse and there was no need for mothers to have alarm for their children, apart from what was happening with the war. Suddenly we heard the air-raid sirens in the distance, then two planes came overhead; one seemed to be chasing the other. Ernie said to me: "Go off home now Peter". I really wasn't listening to his words; I was transfixed by the dogfight overhead as they were diving and twisting all over the sky. There was a very loud bellow behind me: "GET OFF HOME". This frightened me more than anything.

I ran as fast as my little legs could carry me, down to number twenty where we lived. I remember some noise above my head and bits of slate crashing down into the street. I was told years later that it had been bullets from one of the planes, hitting the roof slates. I burst through the front door, (nobody locked their doors in those days), up the lobby, through the living room, into the back kitchen and hid under the stairs. I had forgotten that Mam was still at Auntie Maude's. When she came in and found me, she pulled my shorts down and proceeded to clean me up as the smell from my fright had made it easy for her to find me.

Olympic Dockers

Dad came home and told us about another close shave he and his mates had at work. A ship had been hit; it was lying in the dock and was taking on water. Volunteers were called for to unload the cargo of Aluminium Ingots down in the hold. The fire services were working hard to pump out the water. Dad and his mates were provided with wellington boots, they climbed into a cargo sling, which lowered them into the ship's hold. The water had a green tinge and they fished about with their hands and arms below water, grabbing the ingots and throwing them into slings ready for hoisting. The water level was going down and they were winning the day. Suddenly, Dad spotted the tail fins of an unexploded bomb just breaking the surface and he could clearly hear it ticking or was it his own heart pounding in his chest? He shouted to his mates who took one look before making a mad dash for the ladder. Dad said, he thought they all broke the world record for climbing a ladder that day. The area was quickly evacuated and an Army bomb disposal team came to defuse and make the bomb safe. Those men must be among the bravest people anywhere. Having to sit almost on top a ticking explosive device that could go off at any moment.

Tears of sadness

One cold December night, our little brother Terry passed away, he had caught pneumonia, which was a very common complaint in those days. The causes of respiratory illnesses were due to the conditions that people lived in. During the winter, washing was hung up to dry on a creel over the fireplace or elsewhere indoors. Mothers of large families would struggle all through the winter with this essential task and people were just not aware of the effect this had on the very fabric of a house. Although bedrooms did have their own fireplaces, people could not afford the coal to warm these rooms up. Only once in my young days did I see the luxury of a glowing fire in my bedroom, that was just before I was taken into hospital with pneumonia. Dampness permeated into every corner of every room. Doors and windows were kept tightly closed to keep out the cold; the result was a fungal growth of mould spores either green or black in colour, especially on the outer walls, which were much colder. We all had to sleep in these conditions and the bedclothes often felt damp when we snuggled down for the night. Terry had been a very happy and cute baby and Mam told me later that I couldn't stop crying when he died, I was just a toddler myself but I must have sensed his departure.

War Trophies

Sometime later, I started at infant's school, Canon Kennedy Memorial School in Edge Lane. It was quite a long walk to the school. It was the days before school buses. Very few people had cars and I can remember sometimes having to walk behind dad through a heavy snowfall, holding onto his overcoat flaps, pulling them around my ears to keep out the cold, my nose would be two inches away from his bum. I was five years of age and soon learned the route there and back. It was the norm in those days for kids to find their own way to school. We soon became independent but sometimes, mischievous little buggers.

The War was still on and boys would bring trophies out of their pockets at playtime. Pieces of shrapnel, bullet cases, live bullets, nose cones off shells. Over the next couple of years, I saw a whole range of weaponry including a German Luger Pistol, that one boy had tucked down the front of his pants.

Another boy brought in a small live Mortar bomb that made the schoolteachers go into a state of panic when one of them spotted it. The wardens were summoned and the bomb was placed gently into a bucket of water and taken away. The head teacher gave us all a lecture and forbade us to bring anything else we found, into the school. Everybody was given a gas mask, which we had to carry at all times when we were out and about and wherever we went. They were in a strong cardboard box with our names on and they had a piece of strong string, which we placed over our heads and one shoulder. Every now and then, the teachers made us put them on and parade around the playground to get used to wearing them. We boys thought we all looked like Martians that we had seen in our comics and started to walk with stiff arms and legs until the teachers told us off. We certainly couldn't talk properly in them and the glass eye pieces would steam up so we couldn't see where we were going. There was a little tin of Vaseline in the box, which could be used to smear the insides of the eyeglasses to stop them steaming up, but this was only to be used in an emergency whatever that was. Mam, Dad, my sister and brothers all had their own gasmasks and Mam even had one for the baby that was big enough to put her completely inside. We didn't really know why we had to carry these gas masks and never worried about it. We had the masks hanging around the house for many years after the war had finished. One night when there were several grown ups celebrating something, they were all drinking and smoking their heads off, I put one of the masks on and sat quietly in a corner reading my comic. Eventually, they all noticed me and asked why I was wearing the gas mask. I told them I didn't like the cigarette smoke and it was making my eyes water. I never did take up smoking; the nearest I got to smoking was in the Hippodrome picture house with my mates when I was about fifteen years old. One of them passed me a lit cigarette and told me to inhale, I did and almost burst my lungs in a coughing fit. It was horrible and I felt as though my throat was on fire. Lots of grown up people around us started complaining because I was spoiling their film. The usherettes came and told us to leave. That was the first and last time I ever put a cigarette in my mouth and I have been thankful throughout my life for that loathsome experience which taught me a big lesson. I just wish many of my long lost friends who have died of cancer had learned the same lesson.

Knit one pearl one

We were taught how to knit in the infant school. The trouble was, the wooden knitting needles were all blunt at the ends from kids either chewing them or dropping them on their pointed ends. I always found it frustrating trying to get the needle through the woollen stitches but somehow I eventually managed to pick up the skill and mastered the art of knitting. At the age of nine, I produced a piece of Fair Isle with a very nice pattern. Mam was very proud and had kept it for many years. She was an expert with the needles and produced all our pullovers, scarves, gloves, socks, etc., but the wool she bought came in skeins and had to be rolled into a ball before she could start knitting. This is where we were made to hold out our hands, holding the skein while she rolled the wool up into a ball. After a short while it made our arms ache and they would start dropping. Mam would say 'Don't be soft, its not hurting, pick your arms up' but it was hurting. I found that if I put my elbows on my knees, it wasn't so bad. We all went through this ritual many times during our growing up years and it got to the point where we would all quietly disappear whenever we saw Mam getting her knitting bag out of the cupboard, hoping that you weren't the last one and get caught with the wool. I can still hear her knitting needles clicking away in my head; Dad used to say 'I'm sure she could knit an alarm clock if she put her mind to it'.

Bombsite Playgrounds

Bombsites were our adventure playgrounds. There were so many of them, and all the police could do was place signs in front of them reading, 'DANGER KEEP OUT'. This did nothing to deter us from scrambling through the twisted steel girders and tottering walls, to search for some gem of war memorabilia, which could be swapped in the playground. Shrapnel was a favourite item to collect as some of the jagged pieces had beautiful colours - like those of a rainbow - and they were mysterious objects to young boys. It was many years later when I found, that as a bomb explodes, the high temperatures created, would sometimes produce these beautiful colours on the metal. The war must have been a dreadful time for our parents and all grown-ups alike, not knowing if they or their loved ones would survive the terrible bombing raids. However, to us kids it was all an adventure, we didn't see any danger and most of us thought it was just part of the everyday life of growing up. When searching through bombsites, picking up pieces of shrapnel, especially if it had some dried blood or what looked like bits of human flesh stuck to it, the piece became something a bit special and of a higher value in the bartering negotiations in the corner of the playground. We never gave a thought as to where the jagged piece of metal had been on its terrifying passage from the bursting bomb. The jagged pieces of white hot metal would journey at lightening speed. Twisting and turning through the air, going through brick, plaster and wood before ripping into someone's flesh and terminating its journey among a heap of debris, where it would lie undisturbed until some little boy came along weeks later and found another gem for his collection. To us the consequences of a bomb dropping onto people's property did not exist in our thoughts. As a child, you don't look into the future as adults do. The future to me was my next meal, hunger played a big part in our lives and once fed and the pain of hunger had gone, the world was bright again. If I didn't feel that pain on my way home from school, then I was satisfied and took my time dawdling along and looking in shop windows. However, if the pangs of hunger were there, I would run all the way home, through the front door, into the kitchen where Mam was usually doing something like preparing the evening meal and beg her for a Jam Butty that would keep me going until teatime came around. I was just like all kids of my time who would eat anything that was put in front of us. People couldn't afford to be fussy with their diet. If it was food, then it was eaten and we were glad of it. What's more, there were no overweight people around during the second world war and you only visited the doctor if your complaint was a serious one. Doctor Bracey had his surgery office in Kensington opposite 'Kenny Park'. He knew all his patients by their first names and was highly respected in the neighbourhood. It was no trouble for him to turn out on a cold winter's night to visit a sick patient as our Mam could testify during her many pregnancies.

Uncle Tom

When the air raid sirens started on the evening of the twenty ninth of November 1941, many people had taken themselves into the communal shelter in the basement of Durning Road Technical School, Edge Hill, Liverpool. The basement housed a large swimming pool that had been emptied and was being used as a temporary air raid shelter. In an amazing stroke of misfortune, a parachute incendiary mine had descended from one of the German bombers overhead. The wind caught the parachute just before it landed in the street, causing it to descend at a steep angle. The bomb crashed through a window at pavement level, straight into the mass of people sheltering

Durning Road School

below. The white burning phosphorus contents of the bomb exploded. The people never had a chance. The whole school was soon ablaze. Boiling water and steam from the hot water system and leaking gas made the rescue very difficult. The fire brigade worked all night and it was dawn before rescuers could enter the smouldering ruins. One of Mam's elder brothers, Tom Grant, was one of the first men to crawl inside. It wasn't long before he emerged, holding the charred remains of an infant in his arms. On passing the body to one of his colleagues, it broke into two pieces as he uttered the words "They're all like this". Uncle Tom had been all through the First World War, fighting on the Somme. He had been awarded the Military Medal for bravery when he dashed out, into the line of fire to rescue his wounded Officer. However, nothing had prepared him for the spectacle that he'd just witnessed. He sank to his knees with tears running down his face. Not a sound came from the large gathering of people nearby. One hundred and sixty six women, children and old men had perished; many others had been badly injured. It was Liverpool's biggest loss of life in one single incident but the story had not been published at the time because it would have been bad for the moral of the Nation. Uncle Tom never fully recovered after that experience, mother said a beam had fallen onto his back and injured his shoulder. He withdrew into himself and seemed to lose the will to live.

Just another Hero

Dad had been born in 1901, just days before the end of Queen Victoria's reign. When he was just seven years of age he had been in hospital for nearly twelve months with blood poisoning caused by an injured ankle. It was the days before penicillin and the poison to his system nearly killed him. After an operation, he was left with one damaged foot, which stopped him entering the war as a serviceman. However, I think he should have received a medal for the duty he performed throughout the six years he gave to his country all through the Second World War. The pain he must have endured, walking all those miles to and from his place of work when the trams weren't running. The need to feed his family must have been the driving force. When he retired after forty-seven years of loyal service, he received the princely sum of ten shillings a week pension from the Mersey Docks and Harbour Board, ten shillings being fifty pence in today's money. It grieves me when I read about some Chief Executive Officer or director of some large company being awarded millions of pounds in annual bonus payments, even after a poor performance and the shares of their company have been falling over the previous twelve months. I'm sure most people will think like me and say, 'A bonus should only be awarded for good results'. Its greedy people like those who have contributed to the terrible financial crisis that the world is going through right now.

Miscarriage of Justice

One day while still at junior school, during organised games in the playground, it was my turn to leapfrog over a boy who was bent over with his hands on his knees. Just as I reached the maximum height and with my legs outspread, he lost his balance and collapsed under me and we both had a good laugh over it. A senior teacher, who was not involved with the games, just happened to come through a door and see the final outcome; she summoned me to go immediately to the head's office. I tried to explain it was an accident but to no avail. Standing outside the head's office, I was scared and quite rightly so because I was aware of her reputation. The door opened, without a word being spoken, the Nun grabbed my hand. Her heavy leather strap, which she kept hanging between the folds of her long black habit, was out in a flash, raised high above her head and brought down with such ferocity across the palms and fingers of both hands in turn. The pain was unbelievable. As I walked back to the playground with tears streaming down my face and contusions welling up on my palms, I felt pure hatred in my heart towards such evil people and I was just eight and a half years old.

It was many years later before I was to hear and learn the term "Miscarriage of justice" but on that day, in that school, I knew there was something terribly wrong. I was just a small boy, how could I defend myself against such cruel and inaccurate judgement? That incident which I never forgot was to play a big part in moulding my character in later life.

Mother would send us to get "messages". This was the Liverpool term for shopping; I would spend ages waiting in queues. We couldn't go to another shop because our ration books had to be registered with our local store. Sometimes when I reached

23

the front of the queue, the shopkeeper would say, "Sorry son, we are sold out", of meat or eggs or whatever I had been sent for. I would go home and tell Mam, she would take me back and give the shopkeeper a piece of her mind, and then it was all apologies and the goods would be handed over. I hated those childhood years and was always looking forward to being an adult and being able to stand up for myself in front of those kind of people. There was never anything to look forward to as a kid apart from a birthday or Christmas. Both seemed such a long way away that we would forget them until a day or two before. Preparations for Christmas started on Christmas Eve, it was considered unlucky to start any sooner. Decorations consisted of some coloured paper, cut into strips with scissors, and glued into loops to make chains. We made the glue from flour and water. The coloured paper chains would be hung from corner to corner across the ceiling with drawing pins. Suddenly, our living room took on a whole new perspective, with those few decorations; my world was transformed into something magical. We hung our long stockings from the mantelpiece; each with a note bearing our name, to make sure Santa knew whom he was giving his presents to. A day or two before, we had each written a note to Santa Claus, asking for some special toy, then sent it up the chimney where it would catch fire before it went out of sight. The living room fire was the centre of focus and nothing was put in the dustbin that couldn't be put on the fire. A real living fire is a bewitching and charismatic feature in the living room. I would sit for ages, looking at the flames dancing in a multitude of shapes and listening to the crackles as the coal burnt through. Sometimes a sharp crack sounded as some ancient pocket of gas deep inside the coal escaped in a miniature explosion sending a tiny spark out toward us. Mam brought the tin bath in from the yard and after a good scrub from head to bottom then a cup of hot cocoa we went to bed in new pyjamas. Christmas Eve was the one night of the year when we prayed for sleep. Oh what joy and excitement the following morning when we saw our Xmas stockings that were bulging to burst, pulling out a packet of different coloured plasticine with its distinctive smell. Various small toys, a wind-up clockwork car, a big colouring book, crayons, chocolate bar, boiled sweets, an Orange and down at the bottom of the stocking, a two shilling piece or Florin. The decorations had to come down on the Twelfth Night, this was usually done in a few minutes when we were let loose to grab and tear and screw them all up amid roars of laughter and merriment. The home made trimmings were of no further use, they couldn't be saved for the following year. As time went on, shops would be stocked with more decorative items such as crepe paper, balloons and tinsel and little imitation Xmas trees made out of silver coloured cardboard.

Ack Ack Guns

Even though the war was now over, there was still a battery of Anti Aircraft Guns in Kensington Gardens. A couple of Khaki tents nearby and several soldiers, lazing about on their camp beds. I used to cut through the park on my way home from school and would always stop to admire these big guns with their shiny green paint, and polished brass handles. One day as I arrived, there was nobody about. I thought they had all gone and left the guns behind. This was an opportunity too good to miss. Within seconds, I was sitting on the gun-aimers seat, turning all the handles in reach. The barrel was swinging around in a big arc and elevating at the same time. I was shooting those Jerries out of the sky in good style. Ack-Ack-Ack-Ack, I had all the sound effects going too. I was a superb shot as plane after plane came screaming down in a ball of flame and smoke.

Suddenly, there was a horrible scream behind me - "You Little Bastard". I swung around and there to my horror was a big angry soldier running towards me. I was off like a shot across the park but the pursuer was gaining on me. His legs were much longer than mine were; I was in a terrible state of panic. What is he going to do to me? My mind was racing faster than my body; I could hear his footsteps right behind me. I will never know to this day why I suddenly stopped and curled up into a ball but it did the trick. He went flying right over the top of me and landed in an untidy heap about three yards in front. I sprang up, dodged past his sprawled out body and escaped out of the park and into the throng of shoppers. Behind me in the distance, I could hear loud laughter coming from his colleagues and the shout of "Go on ya soft shite, ya couldn't even catch a kid."

I avoided the park route after that fright and resumed to taking the longer one down Jubilee Drive. This was a very monotonous walk home for a small boy, with nothing to stimulate the mind. I was happy when one day, some schoolmates introduced me to the art of "Legging". Legging is hitching a ride on the back of a vehicle without the driver knowing. There was a cross roads at both ends of Jubilee Drive so all traffic using that route have to stop or slow down at either end. This made it perfect for the legger to find a place to hang on for the journey. Lorries with tailboards where the best, we could just hang on with our hands and place our feet on the spare wheel underneath. Charabanc

Morris '8' 1937

buses where a challenge but not impossible, there was a small rain channel under the back window where I could just get my finger tips into and my toes could find a niche in the recessed number plate. With the side of my face pressed against the bodywork, I'd cling on for dear life. Sometimes, the passengers sitting on the back seat spotted me and started shouting and knocking on the window. I couldn't hear what they were saying, but the bus would come to a stop and I'd have to run. One day as I waited for my lift; a little black car came to a halt. The driver was an old man. At the back of the car was a spare wheel fixed upright and a metal carrier used to carry a picnic basket. This was held upright with a leather strap. Before the car could set off, I undid the strap, lowered the carrier and sat sidesaddle, holding onto the spare wheel. This was the most comfortable ride I ever had and I giggled to myself at the thought of seeing the old man when he arrived home, wondering why he'd not fastened the carrier up properly and the strap hanging loose.

All good things come to an end and mine did the day I fell off the back of a big lorry. It must have been doing over thirty miles an hour when I fell off and landed face down in the middle of the road. I managed to crawl to the side of the road and sat on a small parapet. There was a large hole in my forehead and I was losing serious amounts of blood. My nose and chin were badly scraped, as were my knees, elbows, and hands. My toes had scraped along the road and worn my toecaps away before I finally lost my grip. A pool of blood was forming on the pavement and there was nobody around to help. Traffic in those days was very sparse and it could be another ten minutes before another vehicle came along. I felt awful and was hurting like hell but I had to get walking, pushing myself up, I somehow staggered down to the main road and turned into Kensington. I was aware of women looking shocked as I stumbled past them like an old man, determined to get home. Mam nearly fainted when she saw me but never one to panic; she quickly tore up a clean pillowcase into strips and bandaged me up to stem the blood flow.

By the time Dad came home from work about an hour later, I was cleaned up, patched up and sitting by the fire with a hot sweet drink and a blanket around me. Dad picked me up complete with blanket and carried me nearly a mile to the Royal Infirmary where I received stitches to my head wound and an injection against tetanus and dressings to all my other wounds. Dad sat me on his shoulder once again and was walking up Prescott Street when a car pulled up, the driver gave us a lift the rest of the way. That was the last time I "Legged" home from School. It was becoming a very dangerous activity.

Knocked out cold

I didn't consider myself accident-prone but I must have been as a kid. I did have to go back to that hospital some months later, this time in an Ambulance. It was another organised games period in the playground. We had several teams taking part in a race across the yard; touch a small wall and return. When my turn came, I was the 'last man' on our team and we were lying second place. I was giving everything I had and was neck and neck with the leader of the other team. The girls on the sidelines were at fever pitch. We were running towards the two-foot high wall that held the flowerbed. I was feeling confident that my team and I were going to win as I was just ahead of my rival. Suddenly for no reason, I toppled forward and my head crashed into a corner of the sharp red brickwork of the low wall. My next memory was, I'm in a big field full of flowers. My favourite teacher, Miss Owen, is holding my hand and passing me Cream Soda and sweets. I could hear church bells ringing in the distance. The kite I was hanging onto started lifting me off my feet but Miss Owen grabbed my hand and pulled me gently back down and I felt safe. All the time, I could hear church bells ringing. It was a beautiful day, I was very happy and didn't want it to end. Suddenly, there was a rush of cold air on my face and a stinging sensation in my head. I heard a voice say "Take him straight through to the accident department".

The church bells had been the bells on the front of the ambulance. A couple of weeks later, I was back in school, still nursing a sore and stitched up head, (the new wound was an inch above the previous one). I found out that the boy, who was racing next to me, had been expelled for deliberately tripping me up and causing the accident, I wonder if he has mended his ways.

Very lucky escape

There was still a lot of horse drawn traffic around, driven by Coalmen, Milkmen, Ragmen, and Draymen. My nine lives were running out fast because I got run over by a Horse and Cart while playing in the street. It was our Milkman; Ernie Bradbury who

Grandparents Golden wedding 1943 Author extreme left

they say was drunk and galloping his horse home one afternoon. Someone shouted and I turned around as his horse knocked me on my back. Somehow, It's hooves missed me by inches as it galloped right over me, I could see the big iron shod wheels pass either side of me as I lay there on the Street. Some women were talking nearby, I could hear them screaming at the milkman as he continued towards his yard. One of the women picked me up and within seconds, a whole crowd came out of their houses and gathered around but I didn't have a scratch on me apart from a small bump on the back of my head from hitting the road. I could hear them saying, "God, he must be charmed".

It had been a very strange experience and I had flashbacks for the next couple of years. Every detail came to me, the sound of the wheels and the horse's hooves as they clattered onto the street, I even remember what the underside of the milk float looked like.

Tramcars

During the school holidays, we would play for hours on the main road, -Kensington-. The game we played mostly was rounders and we would only move out of the way to let a Tram or the odd vehicle pass by. It was Ann Ventry's turn with the bat. Her brother Louie stood behind as the backstop but he got too close. She swung around in a big arc and hit him full in the face with the heavy cricket bat we were using. Louie was knocked out cold and someone ran to get his Dad, who was the Landlord of the Royal Arch public house nearby, he carried him home in his arms like a rag doll. Louie soon recovered but he was almost as bad as I was, with having accidents. One day, he ran out of a shop on the opposite side of the road, straight across Kensington and smack into the side of a passing Tramcar. I was watching as he bounced off the vehicle and almost landed on the pavement again. A man picked him up, unconscious once again and carried him over to the pub.

Sometimes, we would put bottle tops on the rails to let the tram wheels flatten them as they went past. I put a penny on the rail about six times in succession and it finished up the size of a half a crown but as thin as a wafer. I loved the trams and the noises they made, as they journeyed back and forth. We would put our ears to the rails and hear when the next one was coming before we could see it. They made a whining noise from their electric motors and a screeching sound from the wheels as they rubbed on the rails, then there were the bells to tell the driver that someone wanted to get off at the next stop. Then came an altogether different sound as the driver applied the brakes, by turning the big handle in front of him around several times. The drivers' seat was supported by a single spindle that fitted into a hole in the floor beneath him. When he started off again, he would move a pointer on the dashboard to different numbers for more speed. When the tram came to a terminus, he would take his seat to the other end and push all the passenger seat backrests into the forward position on his way while the conductor swung the overhead trolley around to the rear end by pulling a rope that tethered it to one end or the other. If it was night-time, all the lights would go out on the tram as soon as he pulled the trolley wheel away from the electric overhead cable. There was a set of controls at each end of the tram. The driver would change the destination indicator by turning a handle above his head showing where the next terminus would be. Every tram carried several boxes of sand underneath the seats. The driver could let sand fall automatically onto the tracks by some means within his cab if he was losing traction on hills. Big blue sparks and flashes came from the trolley wheel above the tram as it crossed the electric junctions overhead. Any passenger could operate the stop bell from anywhere along the tram, by tugging on the long leather strap above their head, The signal for stop was one pull and the conductor gave two pulls for the signal to go. I liked to see them going past in the evenings when they were all lit up and sometimes guessed what number would come next, either the Number 6 to Old Swan or 6A to Knotty Ash or the Number 10 to Longview.

Whenever I went on a tram, I would like to go upstairs for the view.

The River was alive

Sometimes at weekends, when Dad wasn't working, he would take us on the tram to the Pier Head and show us all the ships on the Mersey. We could see the tugboats pushing and pulling the great passenger liners that had sailed in from the United States of America and elsewhere around the world. The tugboats were very powerful and it was great to see and hear them working as they churned up the water, creating big whirlpools in the river. The very large spliced ropes would sing as the strain was taken up when they started to pull the giant ships. The river Mersey was alive with ships and boats of all sizes, the horns sounding off across the city; and the waterfront was a hive of activity. We loved spending time at the Pierhead, there were always lots to

Overhead Railway

Pierhead

see and hear, and at 1pm precisely every day, the One-o-Clock Gun would go off at Morpeth dock in Birkenhead. The sound of the gun, a relic from the Crimean War, would tell Mariners exactly what GMT (Greenwich Mean Time) it was. They could also check visually by looking at the Time-Ball, which fell down a mast at the same time. The One-o-Clock gun began in 1867 and was stopped on 18th July 1969 for economic reasons; the authorities decided that one hundred pounds a year was too much to pay for its upkeep. There are three large buildings at the Pier Head called 'The Three Graces', the Royal Liver Building, the Cunard Building and the Port of Liverpool Building. I remember going into the Cunard building and looking at the fantastic models of ships in glass cases. Some of the models were about twelve feet long and I could only imagine they would be perfect miniatures of the real thing in every way. I was left spellbound by the skills of whoever made them. One Sunday, Dad took us on the overhead railway all the way to Gladstone Dock where he worked. He named every dock along the way from Princes Landing stage at the Pier Head to Seaforth even before we got near the dock where the names could be seen. The overhead

The Dockers' Umbrella

railway was nicknamed the Dockers' umbrella because they could walk the seven miles of docks without getting wet.

The Ice Slide

I had missed my sister Micky and brother Gerald a lot since they went off to Wales as evacuees and was glad to see them home again. My sister Patricia who had died as a baby would have been my next eldest sibling, someone who was nearer my age, someone I could have related to more easily. The gap between Gerald and myself was too big for us to confide with each other and I had no close friend in the family who I could talk and play with. On the other side, I had lost my next younger sibling, little Terry who also died at the age of eighteen months. He would have been my pal, someone close, someone to share my life with, he would have been a good friend to play and laugh with while we rough and tumbled on our shared bed. Someone to whisper and share little secrets with from behind the settee. Mother had two more babies, Irene then Christopher, who were post war babies and benefited from plentiful times and good food. But on the other hand, they both have problems in their mid-lives in trying to keep their weight and body mass index down. So, it makes one think, is it the quality and quantity of food given to babies that determines their eventual size? I on the other hand can eat anything and I never seem to put excess weight on. My elder siblings were growing up fast and were fledging their own wings, they wanted to be free from having to look after young Peter and make sure he didn't get into any trouble. I spent a lot of time being cared for by my Grandparents and Aunties who I loved just as much as my parents. When I was old enough, I was put in charge of babysitting my new younger siblings, Irene and Chris, and enjoyed my new role as defender and guardian.

Mickey, Dad & Aunty Ann

My best friend, Colin Ford and myself would play for hours looking after young Chris, especially in winter when we would make an ice slide in the street. The weather was freezing cold but we were all glowing from running and hurling ourselves onto the frozen ice, balancing on two feet and seeing who could slide the longest. Sometimes we would have a tumble but didn't come to much harm. All the kids joined in and the screams of delight could be heard the length of the street. Everyone had red rosy cheeks as we came off the end of the ice, ran back up the street to take our place in the queue. Then it all came to a sudden stop when a nosy old woman came out with a packet of Saxa Salt; she poured it onto our slide, saying, 'someone's going to get hurt'. We were all devastated, every child headed for their homes with heads dropped down, I could hear the ice cracking behind me as the salt got to work. However, not one kid made a remark against the old lady, we all came from working class families and we all knew about respect for our elders.

A lot of workmen came one day, to renew the road surface of Kensington, which was made of wood. It took weeks for them to lift thousands of hard wooden blocks and renew the road surface with some other material. Lots of people living nearby would come out at night and pinch some blocks from the enormous piles at the side of the road. They were a good source of fuel for their fires as they were hardwood and had been pre-treated with something to preserve them from rot yet kept the flames going in the fireplace. I don't know of any other road that had been surfaced with wood and it can't have been a very safe surface to drive on in wet weather.

A night watchman was on duty every night; he had a little hut with a big brazier and a heap of Anthracite to keep it going in the cold weather. He couldn't keep watch everywhere at once and it was funny to see people sneaking out of some shadow when his back was turned, pinch an armful of blocks and dash back before he turned around. Then the same thing happened at the other end of his view. I don't think he could have done much anyway because he was lame with one leg shorter than the other and it took him all his time just to walk with a boot that had a sole about six inches high. We kids loved to stand around his brazier keeping warm until we heard our mothers' shout, for us to come home.

Although Dad was only a Docker, he was very clever with his hands and he must have had a good brain because he taught himself how to make wireless sets. His first set was, what he called, a 'Cats Whisker' or 'Crystal Set' that could only be heard through a pair of headphones. We were all sitting around the kitchen table one evening while Dad was tuning in to a station all the way from London. He said, "Peggy, bring me your mixing bowl love." He put the headphones inside the empty bowl and suddenly, we could all hear it. All our mouths dropped open, it was the first wireless we'd heard and couldn't understand how the man's voice was coming out of Mam's mixing bowl. I'm always amazed how we remember unimportant and inconsequential little things in life like the name of that early radio station, which was called 2LO.

He progressed onto much better sets with stations coming in from all over Europe.

Growing up

The post war years were a horrible time with everything being rationed and a shortage of money. There were lots more mouths to feed as men returned to their homeland from fighting in far-flung places. I was now seven years old and very skinny, having been in Alder Hey hospital for several months with pneumonia.

Then a month at a convalescent home in Southport where they tried to build me up.

I can remember always being hungry and cold, especially in the winter, because my footwear mainly consisted of either Wellies or pumps (Plimsolls). There just wasn't enough money to buy expensive new footwear every six months or so. We only had one pair at a time and they would soon get worn out. I would never think of pestering my mother for new shoes because I knew she didn't have the money. I would scrounge some cardboard and cut out a pair of inner soles for my shoes, they would feel quite comfortable for a while until the cardboard wore through and I could feel the pavement again through the holes. Then one day I had a brainwave. When nobody was in the house, I pulled Mam's sideboard away from the wall and cut two innersoles out of the linoleum then pushed the sideboard back to hide my foul deed. The linoleum innersoles lasted much longer. Kids always had runny noses and I was no exception. We were lucky if we had a handkerchief. One kid I knew always wiped his nose on the back of his coat sleeve, this resulted in a long silvery coating of dried snot up his sleeve and his nose and top lip were red raw. Sniffing was a sound that could be heard all through the day in the classroom. It was a common sight to see 'candles' going up and down the nostrils as boys were concentrating on their essay.

First Hurdle

My next elder brother Gerald was very agile; he would often run along our lobby and vault over the Baby Gate at the front door in one quick leap. I was much smaller than him and had no chance of doing the same; nevertheless, it didn't stop me trying. I was sitting at the bottom of our stairs, concentrating on the hurdle in front of me, visualising myself as an Olympic athlete, sailing gracefully over the top. After several false starts, I finally gave it all I had and made my leap. Nine tenths of my body made it over but the toes let me down, my face smashed into the hard sandstone flags of the pavement. My two front teeth snapped off and were there amid blood and snot on the sidewalk. I don't remember much after that except sometime later getting the stumps pulled out at the dentist's. I spent the next couple of years being taunted and having people poke fun at my toothless smile, that's when I could raise a smile. Nobody ridiculed me more than my own brother who I had been trying to emulate. The song *'All I want for Christmas is my two front teeth'* haunted me for several years. I couldn't take the ridicule and withdrew into my own little world. I kept to myself and had little confidence; this must have been the reason why I suddenly became a target for bullying. The worst offender was one boy who walked the same way home as me every afternoon; he would start picking on me for no reason. It went on for weeks until someone saw it happening and told my father.

Kensington Boxing Club

In his spare time, Dad was a trainer at the local boxing club; he took me in there the following Sunday morning and spent hours showing me how to use my fists and defend myself. I was fascinated at the way the boxers could use a skipping rope and punch the leather ball on elastic ropes. I had seen girls skipping in the street many times and they were good but these men were absolute masters with a skipping rope. I would watch their boxing boots lifting off the floor in a fascinating rhythmic dance that was too quick for my eyes to see properly, while the rope spun around their body in a blare of vision. As the rope hit the timber floor beneath their feet it made a loud crack and the sound is embedded in my memory, crack-crack-crack-crack, it was almost as quick as a machine gun. They would carry on with their skipping for ages until the sweat rolled down their faces and bodies. Apparently, this was to build up stamina in the bodies. The other strong memory I have, was the smell of a mixture of sweat, leather and carbolic soap which they used in the showers. These aromas greeted everyone as they entered the door of the boxing club. Then there was the sound of metal weights being dropped in the downstairs room. My low-key training went on for weeks and I enjoyed the company of all the men who were involved in the club. One boxer, Nel Tarleton had won the British featherweight title three times. He had received three Lonsdale belts; two of them outright and he brought one to the Kensington Boxing Club and placed it around my waist. Every time he saw me, he would say "Hello Tiger" and throw a couple of pretend punches into my stomach. Nel only had one good lung and he'd also had TB when he was a child but this didn't put him off. At the end of his career, he had lost only twenty out of 145 fights. However, boxing was a hard life and sadly, Nel died two days before his fiftieth birthday in 1956. All this activity and the company of the powerful men at the club gave me more assurance and confidence, which must have shown itself in school because I had no more trouble from bullying. My elder brother Bryan had trained at the same club and was a boxer who had fought at the Liverpool Stadium but he never pursued his hobby after his defeat there.

King Billy's Army

Every year on the Sunday closest to the twelfth of July, the Loyal Orange Lodge annual procession marched along Kensington from the City centre going out towards Prescott Road. It all started with a Dutchman called Prince William of Orange, who came over from across the north sea in 1690 and had a bit of a battle on the banks of the river Boyne in Ireland.

Ever since, there have been celebrations going on every year in commemoration of that battle. It seems an awful long time to eulogise a lot of men killing each other. To us kids though, it was a fantastic sight with all the bands and people dressed in various kinds of uniform. At the head of each band and out in front was the Drum Major wearing long white gloves and carrying a five feet long Mace with a beautiful Scottish design at the top. This would be tossed into the air as he swaggered along twirling it over and over a couple of times and catching it just below the wide decorated head before it hit the ground. Behind him came a row of approximately six or eight side drummers trying to knock holes through their drum skins with their sticks and behind them, an enormously big drum being beaten to death by an equally big man with a black bearskin apron covering his chest and beer belly. Then came the wind instruments, all with puffed out cheeks and going red in the face playing their bagpipes. Both sides of the big drum would be embellished with the name of the particular lodge that the band belonged to. Behind the band came the standard bearers preceding lots of boys and girls dressed in the same colours. The tunes being played are imbedded in my memory to this day, *The Sash My Father Wore* and *Sons of the Sea* among others. Most bands consisted of flautists who were extremely good players. These men were usually dressed in sailors outfits but they never looked smart as a proper sailor would due to the variety of beer bellies and broken noses. It was always a great time for us, a spectacle of pageantry, which lasted for several hours. As we kids grew older, we became aware of an undercurrent of bitterness and hatred across the divide between the Catholics and the Protestant marchers, particularly when they marched past a Catholic Church. The big drum would receive extra punishment and the decibels from the rest of the players increased to fever pitch. Later in the day, the procession would return by the same route. Everyone looked tired, especially the children. Sometimes a drunken lout would throw an empty beer bottle at the big drummer and the police who were always on standby would rush in among the spectators to make an arrest.

Crime and Punishment

The kids in our street were all friendly towards each other; I cannot remember one occasion when there was a fight between any of them. On the other hand, kids from any adjacent street were classed as 'enemy'; we had our territory and they had theirs. There was a sort of pecking order, the further away, the bigger the enemy, so the kids from the next street were just about tolerated. One afternoon, I was walking down the back entry and came across five lads from two streets away; they were coming out of someone's back gate. They told me it was an old lady who lived there, but she had died and her body had been taken away leaving the house empty. I thought it was a bit strange that a whole house with all its contents would be left for anyone to do with what they wanted. The boys were bringing stuff out of the back door and one of them gave me a shoebox with several rolls of bandages and packets of lint. I was very naive and took them home, thinking they would be very useful as I was always skinning my knees and knocking lumps off myself. The following day, a detective came to our house and told Mam that she must take me to the Bridewell in Prescott Street. I was interviewed and accused of being one of the robbers. I didn't know what to say, I had never been in trouble with the Police before. I tried to tell the policeman what had happened and had not robbed anyone but he twisted me around his little finger. Some weeks later, I had to appear with my mother before a juvenile court, where I was fined ten shillings. I found later that two of the boys involved had been sent to a young offender's institution (Borstal); they were serious offenders. I felt ashamed at having brought dishonour on my parents but I really didn't think I'd done anything wrong.

My Dad paid the ten shillings and gave me a smack across the back of my legs with his leather waistbelt when we got home, saying, 'That will teach you not to be so stupid'. It was the one and only time my father ever laid a hand on me and a lesson that was well and truly learned. I am glad to say that was the first and last time throughout my life that I had been in trouble with the law but I do feel sorry for today's kids who grow up with so much temptation around, like alcohol and drugs.

Media magic

On the second of June 1953, Princess Elizabeth was crowned Queen; that was the first time I had seen television. Mrs MacNab had a new television set in her front parlour, which was crowded with neighbours. I stood with other kids on her windowsill looking through the window at a nine-inch black and white TV, showing the royal carriage arriving at Westminster Abbey. I couldn't understand the concept of television and asked how the moving picture could get inside that small box? Gerald my elder brother said, "The pictures come through the air" and I remember looking with mystery at the sky, saying, "I can't see any pictures up there". It wasn't long after, when most people, including us, had a TV. It became a status symbol to have the big aerial in the shape of a letter H on your roof. Prior to the TV, we had become good listeners to the wireless and looked forward to the plays and programmes that were broadcast every evening. We developed good imaginations at an early age and could visualise what was going on through the spoken word. The sounds of doors opening and closing, or a horse galloping down the lane or rain and thunder added another dimension. It was all spoiled for us when television came and showed how someone using two halves of a Coconut shell would create the sound of horse's hooves and someone standing near the microphone waggling a piece of sheet steel to create the thunder. I think the television producers did that on purpose to turn the public off radio, which had a massive following. The radio commentators at sports events were far better than today's. It takes a special kind of skill to describe a tennis match for the radio listener and there was no need to go to a soccer match, we could see every ball that was kicked in our minds eye. However, one programme had us all mystified and which we can look back on with much amusement today, was 'Educating Archie' by Peter Brough, the Ventriloquist. The whole idea of ventriloquism is to watch and listen to the dummy while also noticing whether the ventriloquist's lips are moving or not. We never gave this any thought while listening to the programme on radio. It was a very successful series that eventually had an audience of over ten million people. Every Saturday night, Dad would ask us to be quiet while he got the football results off the wireless. His dream of winning the 'Treble Chance' and a jackpot of £75,000 on the football pools was with him for many years. We all grew up experiencing the weekly ritual of silence all around the house while he recorded the results on his Littlewoods or Vernons coupon. The wireless announcer's voice rising or lowering, depending on the score, "Accrington two, Walsall Three" the last two words would be in a higher pitch, or if the score was lower, i.e. Accrington two, Walsall one" the last two words would be in a lower pitch. This went on all through the fixtures and we could almost guess the scores by the announcer's tone. Apart from a few little wins of a couple of pounds here and there, his dream eluded him but he did have some good fun over the years with his fantasies and how he would change the world when his big win came. Littlewoods Football Pools was the forerunner of Littlewoods plc, the largest family owned firm in the United Kingdom, with shareholders investments valued at nearly one thousand million pounds. It was founded by John Moores in 1923 and became a massive empire and our dad, along with millions of other dads, all with their own dreams, helped them on their way. I once

44

read a story about becoming wealthy. The author, an ex con said, "You will always have money if you remember these three little words, 'Stick em up'." He was only joking of course, as he went on to say, making crime pay and getting away with it is like winning the pools, it's just a dream that only comes true to a tiny fraction of the world's population.

The last 'Legg'

Dad had a garden allotment in Thomas Lane, Knotty Ash where he spent many hours of his free time growing vegetables to supplement the dinner table. I would often go with him to help in some small way, like pulling up potatoes and carrots and piling stuff onto the compost heap. Other gardeners would sometimes give me the odd apple or pear they had grown in their own allotments. On one or two occasions, during the summer holidays, I caught the tram, went there on my own, and spent many happy hours messing about in dad's allotment and chatting to his neighbours. Dad would be working overtime and had no idea where I was. One Sunday afternoon, I found I'd lost my return fare through a hole in my pocket. After searching everywhere, my only option was to 'Legg' the long journey home on the back of a tram. Out in the countryside, the tram tracks were shielded on either side by a long privet hedge. As people were boarding at Knotty Ash, I sneaked onto the 'Cowcatcher' and bumper at the rear and kept a firm grip onto the trolley cord. It was an exhilarating ride as the tram hurtled along between stops and I was making good headway towards home. At Old Swan, the tram came to a halt halfway across a large open junction and the sound of the electric motors died away. I never gave it much thought and assumed we would be on our way anytime now. I had been travelling most of the way with my eyes closed due to the dust that had been blowing up into my face. A strange feeling came over me of someone watching as I sat there clutching onto the rope, then slowly opening my eyes, saw both the driver and conductor standing with their hands on their hips staring down at me. Once again, I was off like a shot, running to break all records across several sets of tramlines, dodging past moving vehicles with the sounds of "Come here you little bastard" ringing in my ears once again. I hadn't realised at the time that the trolley wheel, which picks up the electric current overhead, had jumped the points as a result of my tugging on the rope. It was a long walk home from Old Swan, and I never mentioned where I'd been all day and vowed to myself not to ride on the back of any more vehicles.

Our Micky

We lived in a rented, three bedroom terraced house where I shared the back bedroom with my big sister Monica, she was eight years my senior. Often, when she was getting ready to

Mickey aged 18

go out, I would be fascinated just watching her put her make-up on, especially when she spat into a little box of black stuff, rubbed a small brush up and down the contents a few times, and painted it onto her eyelashes. Then a black pencil was used to highlight her eyebrows, leaving them in a different shape than they already where. After a long time, her face would be painted up and I wondered what it was all for? When she couldn't get hold of a bottle of leg-tan, she sometimes, mixed some cocoa powder or a little gravy browning with some water, and rub it all over her legs. When it was dry, she would get me to draw lines down the backs of her legs with the same eyebrow pencil. I'd have to use my school ruler to get them straight. She told me it was very difficult to buy silk stockings and the leg tan was a good substitute. When silk stockings did become available, they didn't seem to last long before they became laddered so the leg tan was preferred, as it was much cheaper. I don't know why they needed to show their legs anyway, they'd have been better off wearing trousers.

Micky's bedroom always had a different smell than anywhere else in the house, from all the little bottles of cosmetics and boxes of face powder. There were also her items of clothing and underwear she had hanging from various nooks and crannies. There was only one wardrobe in the house and that was in Mam and Dad's bedroom. Bryan and Gerald who shared the front bedroom had a small chest of drawers to keep their clothes in, their suits and shirts hanging from the dado rail around the room.

I always loved my big sister because she would talk to me as she was getting ready and ask me how my schooling was going on, and then she would give me little snippets of advice. We all called her Micky instead of Monica, I don't know why; it seemed to suit her better. She was and still is a loveable character who nobody could fall out with. When you're in Micky's company, you always have a smile on your face from her personal accounts of everyday life, which somehow never happen to ordinary folk. One funny incident that happened many years later, was when she made a telephone call to a local radio chat show on Merseyside. She had prepared herself by putting a little tape recorder by the wireless to record the interview. When she played it back, the sounds of the voices was very slow and drawled she realised that the batteries in the recorder were wearing down. A quick dash to the shops for new batteries, back home, batteries inserted and all excited as her husband 'Mac' arrived home from

Mac

work. "Mac, listen to this, I've been on the radio today." She switched on, unaware of the mysteries of electronics, Mickey had recorded her three minutes of fame in very slow time as a result of the weak batteries. Now, with strong batteries, the recorder was replaying at normal speed but the sounds coming out of the machine made her and the interviewer sound like a couple of fast talking chipmunks and not a word could be understood. Big Gordon, nicknamed 'Mac', a Liverpool taxi driver and an equally loveable and placid character who never lost his temper, had been listening patiently, then turned around and said, "Very nice girl, now where's me friggin tea?" The rest of the household were cracking up with laughter.

Sometimes, my big sister would take me with her when she visited her friend Eileen Davies at her home in Kensington Street. For some reason, I never enjoyed being there. Mr. Davies had a firewood delivery business that he operated from home. Bundles of sticks were put into a small metal press, a handle was pushed down, which squeezed the sticks together and a rubber band made from old inner tubes, placed around them to keep the sticks together. The deliveries were done on an old handcart, which was chained up to the railings at night outside their front door. Looking back, I think Micky took me with her to carry the bundles of firewood home that Mam had sent her for. Mr. Davies, a previous Rag and Bone Merchant, started another little business, making and selling Toffee Apples. I would visit the house more often then, to buy one for a penny. You had to be careful not to get a splinter in your mouth from the rough wooden sticks he used to push inside the apple as a handle. I was sure the wood came from his firewood business. They had a large family, the youngest was Terence who was about six or seven years younger than me. He showed me down to the cellar where they all worked, sawing, chopping and bundling the sticks together. There were lots of old floorboards that had come from bombsites around the area and wooden boxes Mr Davis got from the market. Although I liked Mrs Davies, and her children who were really nice to me, I was always glad to leave that house which seemed very sparse and felt unloved. Young Terry, known as Bud, showed me a large hole in the living room door where his Dad had punched his fist through the night before, in one of his tempers.

Terry, one of ten children grew up to be a film director and producer. One of his films, 'Distant Voices, Still Lives' was a true story about his family. My sister Monica (Micky) and her friend Eileen; Terry's sister and another two friends were all portrayed in the film and played by real actresses.

Micky left home at the age of eighteen to work as a waitress in Butlins Holiday Camp at Pwllheli North Wales. Mam moved into the back room with Irene the baby, the bedroom that Micky and I had been sharing. Dad had the middle bedroom to himself, which was a good move on mother's part as it left little opportunity for her to become pregnant again. I moved into the front bedroom with my big brother Bryan who had just come back from Honk Kong. He started working in his old job as a rat catcher for Liverpool Corporation but it wasn't long before he left them and started work as a navvy, digging trenches. I was shocked one morning when I saw his face, which had been terribly battered. Apparently, he had been out drinking the night before and got into a fight outside the Locarno Ballroom. Fighting was something that he continued to do throughout his life, he had a very short temper and was the only member of our family who seemed to attract trouble that way, the only way he could answer, was with his fists. He called it 'Male Rutting' and thought that was how all men should conduct themselves.

Home made fun

Unlike today's kids, some having many hundreds of pounds worth of toys and electronic equipment at their disposal, we had very little and got most of our enjoyment from everyday objects found laying about the house. For instance, two empty tin cans and a length of string to make a telephone. One of my friends would walk across the street with one of the cans and talk into it, the idea was, his voice would be carried along the string and come out in the can I was holding to my ear. It kept us amused for some time but the tin can telephone only worked if the string was kept taught. Another use for tin cans was stilt walking. This time, a loop of string was attached to each can and we balanced onto them, keeping the string held tight with our hands and clip clop up and down the street on them. We would have races between the boys and girls and sometimes the neighbours would come out to see what all the noise was. Ten or twelve kids running up and down the street on tin can stilts created one hell of a racket. One of my favourite toys was the bicycle wheel rim. We would get an old bike wheel and take away all the spokes and hub, including the worn out tyre and innertube. With just the bare metal rim and a piece of stick, we would run up and down the street and around the corners, using the stick to whip it faster and faster. This too was a noisy toy and by dextrous use of the stick, the wheel would be steered around corners, people, and objects such as pillar-boxes and lampposts. The wheel rim became our personal transport and we wouldn't think of going anywhere without it. One day, my elder brother Bryan was asked to go to the cobblers opposite the Casino picture house to pick up a pair of Mam's shoes that had been in for repair. It was quite a distance and he ran all the way, whipping his wheel rim along Kensington main road and arrived in a lather of sweat. When he came out of the shop, he found somebody had nicked his wheel and he immediately went into a state of panic as to how he was going to get home without his 'personal transport'.

Then there was the home-made steering carts that consisted of a piece of old wooden plank, four pram wheels and a piece of washing line to steer it with. We had many hours of fun pulling them up to the top of Romilly Street, which was the only inclined street in the area. Then hurtling down to Fielding Street, taking the sharp corner at the bottom on two wheels and more often than not, coming to grief when the cart overturned and we would graze our knees or elbows once again. The 'steeries' as we called them would be very useful for fetching a bag of coal from the coal merchant or helping Mam on her weekly trips to and from the public wash house in Balm Street with her enormous bundle of washing.

If we could scrounge the wood and nails, we would make some stilts. They would only raise us up about two feet off the ground but it felt an awful lot higher. We could peep in through people's fanlights over their front doors. One night, I borrowed and got dressed up in my Dad's big overcoat and trilby hat then knocked on someone's door. Florrie Ford nearly died of fright when she opened it and saw the very tall figure in front of her, she screamed and I fell backwards off the stilts. Colin, her son who was my mate, had been hiding in the shadows, burst into laughter, it was he who had put me up to it.

Another use for a tin can was to make a winter warmer. We would punch a lot of holes in the can with a hammer and six-inch nail and attach a long piece of electric wire in the shape of a loop. Then fill the can with paper, wood, & coal, and set it on fire, then swing it around in a big circle to fan the flames. Sometimes a wire would come undone or burn through and the can of flaming embers would go hurtling through the air at a terrific speed, frightening the life out of some innocent passer by. It was nearing Guy Fawkes Night, I had a few penny bangers and thought I would see how loud a bang I could make. Fastening three together with an elastic band and twisting all the blue touch papers together, I lit them and dropped them into the empty dustbin in the back yard. BOOM they made one hell of a bang and the bin lid flew off. Then there was another noise, a crashing sound followed by a muffled curse coming from the kitchen. I walked up the yard, looked in through the half glass door, and saw dad lying on his back on the kitchen floor. A four inch paint brush in one hand and a quart tin of white gloss paint in the other with the contents spilling all over his chest and running down onto the floor. He had been balanced with one foot on a dining chair and the other on the edge of the dresser painting the ceiling when he thought 'Gerry' had come overhead again on another bombing raid. I sneaked out of the backdoor and kept out of the way for a couple of hours. When

I did come in, they didn't have a clue it was me who caused the bang, they all thought somebody's gas stove had blown up.

Street Life

Every November the fifth, we had a big bonfire in the middle of the street. Sometimes, a three-piece suite would appear ready to go on the fire, which was considered better quality than the one somebody already had. So a quick recovery was made and their older one substituted. Then before the fire was lit, someone else would take that one away and bring their much older one out to burn. It was a very dangerous time for youngsters to be out and about when the fire was lit as young men had no sense of safety, some of them were absolutely dangerous and fireworks would be flying all over the place. My brother Bryan saw someone holding a rocket in his hand and lighting the blue touch paper before aiming it along the street over people's heads. He thought he would do the same but held it by the stick instead of the body of the rocket, he ended up with the skin being burned off the back of his four fingers, they looked horrible and it must have hurt him a lot. Later in the evening as the fire subdued, people who came out of the pubs after the ten o'clock closing would sit around the dying fire talking and laughing. Some would put big King Edward potatoes into the embers to cook; they tasted delicious sprinkled with a bit of salt. Talking about food, our local Chippy, as well as selling beautiful cod, haddock, skate and halibut, sold pigs feet, tripe, home made fish cakes and scallops.

Fish and chips cost six pence and a bag of chips in newspaper was just two pence. They used lard and dripping to fry all their goods and they tasted wonderful sprinkled with copious amounts of salt and lashings of vinegar. I was waiting in the

Chippy one night during a power cut. The owner had several candles burning to illuminate his shop. The big frying range that was heated by gas was still in full operation and I spotted one of the big candles slowly tipping over then disappearing into the hot fat among the chips. I seemed to be the only one who saw what happened but didn't mention it and thought it wouldn't really matter as it was made of the same sort of stuff anyway.

At the top of our street was a grocery and bread shop called 'Scotts'. Sometimes they would forget to fold the big window blind away at night and I would jump up, grasp one of the metal bars, and swing back and forth like a trapeze artist. I was doing just this one evening when I felt an almighty whack on my backside which stung like hell. Dropping to the ground I saw a big policeman standing over me, he had hit me with his rolled up cape. *'Get off home before I lock you up'* he said and I ran like the wind. I dare not tell my parents at the time and that's how it should be today. The old fashioned policemen kept us on the straight and narrow and we grew up with a healthy respect for law and order.

One of my personal hatreds on today's life is litigation. Too many people are seeking compensation as a result of the Law Society advertising every day on television. *'Where there's blame, there's a claim'* is one advert that has been running so long, it's on everyone's lips. This claiming culture has created a society who is scared to chastise an unruly child. The children of Britain are aware of this, resulting in the problems we have today.

Unholy Smoke

It was another two years before I got fitted up with new teeth. I was treated at the Liverpool School of Dentistry and my appointments were always during lessons so it was something

I looked forward to. The trainee dentist who treated me was a young lady who seemed to take me under her wing and made me feel special every time I arrived. Over a period of several weeks, she fitted me up with my new denture and a gold filling that I have to this day. I was with her as she drew the small amount of precious metal from the store and watched her as she smelted the gold in a small tabletop furnace then pour it into the mould. We went back to my dentist's chair, one of about fifteen in a long row facing an equally log row of windows, where she fitted the shiny filling into the prepared cavity in my mouth. When I got back to school, I was the new kid on the block, and everyone wanted to see my new gold tooth. I felt like a film star and I was just thirteen years of age.

Dad was quite a religious man and made sure we all went to church on a Sunday morning. Sacred Heart Church at Mount Vernon would be packed to the door at the eleven o'clock mass, which was nearly an hour long. Sometimes I would get dizzy and feel light headed, I think this was due to the smell of incense and the constant droning of prayers being said by the multitude of people.

After mass, on our way out, Dad would sometimes talk to the priest who had a strong Irish accent. 'Now then Mr Kelly, you have some good children and I'm glad to see them following the faith, I think its about time young Peter gave some help at the Altar'. The following week, I was dressed in a purple Cassock and white ruffled collar, assisting one of the younger priests at the earlier nine o'clock mass. After a few weeks I progressed to swinging the burning incense holder but that only happened the once because I dropped the thing and spilt all the burning charcoal over the altar steps.

Then the following week, I did the same with the holy water as I was pouring it over the priest's hands. Father Delayney's hopes of me entering the church were quelled and I was glad, I knew it wasn't the life for me.

Weather Monitor

My secondary education at Sacred Heart School, Mount Vernon seemed to fly by. I learned two of the three 'Rs' - reading and writing. How to make a dovetail joint in wood, how to swim and little much else. There were forty-eight boys in our class. Mr. Saunders, our teacher, would draw something on the blackboard and say "Get on with it". He would then lift his big desk lid and disappear behind it. He too was a person who ruled with the rod and whoa betides anyone who made a noise. We spent many hours in total silence, either daydreaming or doodling; one or two bright boys who sat at the front would get help with their lessons. We all watched in amazement one day when a big boy, who had been brought out to the front of the class to receive punishment, grabbed the cane out of the teacher's hand and belted him over the face with it. He ran out of the school and we never saw him again. Mr Saunder's face was livid when he heard one or two of the class making sounds of approval. We were all made to stand in line while he gave every one of us an extra special whack across our left hand with his cane. Sitting back down, we had to carry on with the essay we were writing while opening and closing our left hands under the desk to ease the pain. I don't know how it happened but I was given the job of weather monitor. At half past nine every morning, I would leave my desk, walk to the wall behind Mr Saunders and take the thermometer out into the playground where I had to swing it around a few times to get a reading. Then return and record the day's temperature onto a wall chart. One morning I saw what Mr Saunders was doing behind his desk, he was reading his morning paper and must have been thoroughly absorbed because he didn't notice me watching. I was able to tell all the lads at playtime about his habit. Some of them told their parents and a few days later, one of the parents came to the school and reported him to the headmaster. The headmaster's office was directly behind our teacher's desk, the walls of his office were only about seven or eight foot high. We all had a grin on our faces one morning when we saw the headmaster, Mr Tighe's head popping over the top, watching Mr Saunders reading his paper. For some reason, we had a new teacher a few weeks later. I found it very difficult to understand maths and remember once, trying to get my head around the decimal point but to no avail. I often felt very foolish and inadequate and it was much easier for most of us to keep quiet and look forward to our fifteenth birthday and going out into the big world of employment.

The Headless Cyclist

I did get a part time job before leaving school, delivering accumulators to people's houses. These were lead and acid batteries that were needed to power wireless sets. They were made of glass, with a strong carrying handle and were very heavy. I would take them around on a bicycle; having threaded the carrying handles onto the handlebars. I couldn't get more than four at any one time on the bike, as it would have been impossible to steer. Old people wanted me to connect them up which was a simple task, the red connector to the plus sign and the black connector to the minus sign. I would bring the dead ones back to the shop for recharging and connect them all up to the charger in parallel.

One day, I was riding my bike along Kensington and came across a crowd of people standing in a group at the side of the road. I leaned the bike up against a shop window and edged in through the crowd to see what was going on. A man's body was laying in the gutter but he didn't have a head, then I saw a big lorry nearby that was carrying big sheets of steel some of the sheets had come loose and were hanging over the edge of the lorry. The man's head was lying further along in the gutter. He had been riding a bicycle when the lorry went past and the steel sheeting decapitated him.

I couldn't understand what the black slimy stuff was that was coming out of the mans neck along with all the other stuff and heard someone say, "It's tar from his lungs, he must have been a heavy smoker". I was more shocked by the tar than anything else. It looked horrible.

Discovering Girls

Puberty took a hold when I was about fourteen, girls all of a sudden looked different to my mates and me. Instead of playing the usual games of hide and seek or tag, they became objects of discovery and exploration and they started smelling different, quite nice smells like Micky's paraphernalia in her bedroom. There was a long passageway between Fielding Street and Phythian Street, which we nicknamed, The Seven Jiggers because it had seven turns and was ideal for cuddling and canoodling. Apart from a lot of snogging while trying to learn the mysteries of the bra strap with one hand and coming home with sore lips, none of us knew what we were supposed to do, but at the time, it seemed to be better than tear-arseing around the streets on one roller-skate. Nevertheless, pretty soon, most of us tired of this new experience and went on to more adventurous activities like seeing who could ride a bicycle backwards the furthest. By sitting on the handlebars and glancing over my shoulder, I could ride up and down every street around the area without stopping. We went on to creating a cinder cycle track at the back of the park and would race around at high speed for hours.

Only two people in our street had cars, Mr Jones, the plumber and Mr Cummins the French polisher. Mr Cummins had two daughters who went to grammar school; they were always smartly dressed and obviously lived a better life than most. Veronica the eldest became a good friend of mine and would sometimes invite me to tea on Sunday afternoons. I got the impression that her parents encouraged the friendship so they could keep an eye on her; after all, we were only fifteen and lived opposite each other. Veronica was a very pretty girl who would soon become a young woman, so it was in her parents' interest to keep her from wandering. The two tradesmen mentioned were the only householders in the street with private telephones; our nearest public phonebox was along the main road, outside Stevens, the chemist's shop. Most kids couldn't pass a phonebox without going in and pressing button 'B' to see if any money came out. To use a phone, you had to deposit four old pence in the slot and dial the number. When you got a connection, you pressed button 'A' but if there was no answer, you pressed button 'B' to get your money back. Kids would push some paper up into the slot to stop the money falling out, then come back later to retrieve what they hoped to get. All telephone boxes had a large directory on a little shelf, and nobody thought of destroying them. The words graffiti and vandalism weren't heard of, well not around our way. The only reason for people to get annoyed with us was walking along the tops of their backyard walls. It was an adventure to walk all the way to Kensington along the back walls, which were about two and a half metres high. Some of them had shiny pointed bricks on the tops, but this didn't stop me, and I became good at balancing, like a circus performer. Neither my mates nor me ever considered breaking or defacing anything. All this was in a big city, unlike so many of today's cities and towns, where mindless yobs wreak havoc around their own homes and turn them into ghettos unfit for decent people to live in. Our misdemeanours were all low key and innocent.

Beached Whale

Before the 'Overhead Railway' was pulled down, our school decided to take us on one last trip to show those kids who had never been on it what a wonderful piece of heritage we were losing. It just so happened that our eyes also had a treat from the sight of a massive ship that was lying on its side in a dock. The SS *Empress of Canada*, previously known as the *Duchess of Richmond*, was a cruise liner that was berthed in Gladstone Dock when it caught fire. The fire service pumped so much water into it, trying to put out the massive blaze that the 20,022-ton ship capsized. From our vantage point on the railway platform at Seaforth, we all looked down into the dock and gazed in awe at the enormous size of the ship lying on its side like a beached whale. Eventually after nearly a year and with the use of lots of 'Donkey Engines' fastened to the quayside, the hulk was brought upright inch by inch. It was towed to Italy where it was cut up for scrap. I thought at the time, 'All those preparations of making it water tight, pumping the water out, bringing and fastening down lots of giant winch engines, fastening lots of steel hawsers to the ship, then afterwards, towing it all the way to Italy to cut up for scrap. Why didn't they cut it up where it was?'

My school days came to an end at fifteen years of age and how happy I was to get away from the place, which I considered a complete waste of time, especially in the latter years when nothing new was taught. To take time up, the teacher got into the habit of reading to us in the afternoons. He tried with the classics, authors such as Francis Bacon and Charles Dickens.

We thought they were a dead loss; nobody was interested so he read us the story, The Invisible Man by H.G. Wells, which we found far more appealing. It was years later before I realised why he read these stories to us. Just after the war, there was a big shortage of written material; in fact, there were very few books in the whole school. There was a massive shortage of goods and everything that was being produced was made as cheaply as possible. The post war goods were called UTILITY BRAND and had a logo which looked like two fruit pies each with a piece missing. Our school exercise books were made of very rough paper. We got into the habit of scratching off pieces of sawdust and wood chippings that were embedded into the page before attempting to do any writing. Otherwise the pen nib could catch on one of them and flick ink all across the page, just when we were coming to the end of an essay. Whatever happened, it didn't really matter at the time because I had no qualifications. My education had suffered as a result of so much absenteeism through ill health and long stays in hospital. Injuries to my head and visits to the dentist didn't help. Then there were the disinterested teachers who must take some of the blame. I was just unfortunate to be born in the wrong era. When I left school, little did I know that I was now entering the biggest learning academy in the world, The University of Life.

'Sorry Girl, it's seen better days'

I found a job as a pawnbroker's assistant opposite Holt Road in Kensington. Hewsons was a large household goods shop that sold small pieces of furniture, rugs, crockery plus cutlery, linoleum, fancy goods and a whole range of jewellery and clocks. The pawnbroking business was at the rear, where customers gained access via the back alley - or back entry, as they are known on Merseyside.

Jim the pawnbroker was a rotund figure, dressed in a crisply ironed light brown warehouse coat that had faded with many visits to his wife's washtub. He always wore collar, tie, and his shoes shone to perfection. Although he was an employee himself, it was he who interviewed me for the job and I was chosen because I was deemed the neatest writer out of all the applicants.

My so-called skill was put to the test the following Monday morning. I had to be dressed in a suit and tie and Jim showed me to a large sloping desk and high chair, just like the one I had seen in the film 'A Christmas Carol' where Bob Cratchit sat and worked. My first task was to set a date stamp with the correct date, and stamp a big pile of tickets twice, once on the ticket and once on the counterfoil. When the doors to the entry were opened at 9.30 a stampede of women rushed into the place, bearing parcels and bundles of all sizes under their arms. Jim raised his voice and asked them to calm down. They had been waiting in the back jigger for the doors to open and had been swapping all the gossip from the weekend. Jim took the first parcel, placed it on the lino covered counter desk in front of him and examined the contents with the eye of an expert. "Five shillings, Mrs Jones," he would say. "Arre come on Jim, its worth more than that," came the reply. "Sorry girl, it's seen better days." "Five shillings for Mrs Jones, one parcel of bedding," he would call out to me. As this banter was going on, I would be writing out the first of many pawn tickets, complete with counterfoil and with the customer's name and amount loaned. I would slide the complete ticket along the counter to Jim and he would tear off the counterfoil, which he pinned to the bundle or garment, then open his big cash draw with wooden bowls inside that contained different denominations of coinage, and pay the lady the five shillings.

Two other lads worked in the pawnshop as well as me. They were not required to wear a necktie; they were the storers and fetchers. Tommy and Eric's job was to take the pawned items to the upper floors and put them in their respective places. As the morning progressed, the lads became a lather of sweat from running up and down two flights of stairs with arms full of men's suits, ladies and gents coats, shoes and bundles of washed and ironed bed linen or table cloths etc. Maybe even, canteens of cutlery. The amount and variety of objects that people borrowed money on surprised me. There were brass fender boxes, old swords, companion sets and even a box of false teeth upstairs with labels tied to each set.

[The Pawnbroking or pawnshop banking business originated in Lombard Italy under the name of Lombard banking by medieval merchants. They hung a symbol in front of their houses, which showed three balls suspended from a bar to attract attention. In more modern times, Pawnbrokers (and their detractors) jokingly refer the three balls to mean "Two to one, you won't get your stuff back".

Mondays and Tuesdays were the busy times for taking goods in. Wednesday morning was a day for sorting out the stockrooms. Jim would look at all the goods and their tickets and if anything was over three months old, officially it had passed its redemption date. This was the date when customers had to collect their goods, by paying a percentage on the amount borrowed, but Jim never stuck to that date. It was more like six months when the items were taken down to the pawnshop where he would put a price on it for sale. If it was a man's suit and it was a nice day, it would be put on display outside the shop in Esher Road where it was placed high up above people's heads with the use of the long pole we had for opening the shop window blinds. Second hand shoes for sale would be hung on hooks just above head height inside the pawnshop. Everything had a large enough price tag that people could read without squinting too much. The upper storeys smelled very strongly of camphor from the thousands of mothballs in every nook and cranny. Manmade materials had either not been invented or where in their infancy. The hundreds of woollen suits and long coats were a breeding ground for the tiny female moth who happened to fly in through an open window and lay her eggs in the folds of someone's best Sunday outfit. Once the grubs had hatched they had a ready meal of pure wool to munch on for a few weeks until it was their turn to fly off into the big wide world. I have seen the results and sometimes a garment would be ruined, looking almost like a net curtain.

Gold rings, watches and jewellery were kept in either of two big safes. As my time progressed, Jim taught me how to deposit and retrieve precious items from the safes, I remember being very impressed by the quality of workmanship that went into making them. Behind the two massive steel doors, which were an art in themselves and beautifully decorated outside and in, there were lots of rich wooden draws with countersunk and flush fitting brass handles. The polish on the wood was superb and the gaps between the drawers and the surrounding wood was so fine it left me wondering about the very skilled men who produced such quality work. They would have learned their trade as apprentices and spent many years perfecting their skills to a very high degree. However, modern times and progress were on the way, and all that would change.

Most of the women customers would come back again on Friday or Saturday to retrieve their husband's best suit or shoes ready for him to wear at the weekend. Lots of their husbands had no idea where their clothes had been all week. I soon became aware of one woman who was rather posh but short of money. She would make a telephone call every Tuesday afternoon and Jim would ask me to write a ticket out. I would have to take the shop bike to her house in a road full of large Victorian dwellings with long front gardens. I'd give her the ticket and two-pound notes and she would give me the parcel containing her husband's suit. Friday afternoons saw me taking the suit back again and collecting the two pounds plus the interest; I cannot remember what the percentage was for borrowing. The shop bicycle, with its big heavy metal frame on the front that contained a large basket, was very awkward to ride. The front wheel was much smaller than the rear, to make room for the basket. Under the crossbar was a steel plate that advertised the shop name and telephone number. The whole thing was quite heavy and ungainly to ride and you could see lots of similar bikes all over the city; it was a cheap way of delivering the goods.

One Friday afternoon, a woman came in with her ticket and pleaded with Jim to let her take her husband's suit; she promised she would come in on Saturday morning to pay. She explained that her hubby needed his suit for a function on Friday night but she wouldn't get his wages until Saturday. "Sorry Mrs, no loot, no suit". He said.

"Oh friggin hell, he'll kill me if his suit's missing tonight," she cried. She never got the suit and we never saw her again. We did see Jim reading the *Liverpool Echo* with a new interest after that.

When the pawnshop was quiet, I would work in the front shop as a sales assistant. The staff consisted of old Mr Hewson, his son and two senior salesmen, Arthur and Stanley. These last two had worked there before they were called up into the army; I loved to hear about their exploits during the war. Arthur had been a paratrooper involved in the fighting at Arnhem. He brought quite a few war souvenirs into work to show us. Among others, was a beautifully made dagger with a swastika on the handle and a pair of field glasses that he had taken off the body of a German officer. As a boy, I was spellbound by such stories and trophies and had desires of being a soldier myself.

There were also two women who worked in the shop; young Mr Hewson's wife and a younger woman called Elizabeth who tended the jewellery counter. One afternoon she let out a terrific scream, and wet herself after a man came in and asked to see some rings from the window display. She left the card full of rings on the counter, when he asked to see some more further to the front of the window.

While leaning into the window, she caught the attention of a nice man walking passed who gave her a smile and a big wink. Elizabeth came over all starry eyed and the blood rushed to her cheeks. It was only when she got back to the counter that she realised the man was her customer who was now gone and so was the card full of expensive signet rings.

The poor girl was obviously very naïve and was in shock for the rest of the afternoon.

She had a second fright some weeks later when she left the bank with some small change she'd been sent for. A young guy snatched the parcel out of her hands and ran like the wind. He got away with ten pounds in pennies, halfpennies, and some threepenny bits. I had to accompany her every time, after that episode.

One very memorable incident happened on a Saturday afternoon when I was told to go outside and close the window blinds. It was nearly six o'clock when I took the long heavy pole outside and guided the hook into the hasp on the front of the first blind. These blinds were very large and heavy and it took all my strength to push and let them roll back into their frame above the big windows. The first one went in ok and slapped into its box frame with a bang, but on doing the second one, it stopped rolling at the halfway point. I pushed but it wouldn't go any further, so I gave it a tug back open but it wouldn't move that way either. All this time, the pavement was busy with people moving one way or the other. Gripping the pole firmly, I gave it a heavy tug and the whole of the blind complete with the heavy steel roller came out of the recess towards me. I was thrown off balance backwards, the pole in my hands loosened itself from the hasp and went backwards over my head, and I heard a smash of broken glass as the heavy hook end hit the windscreen of a passing taxi. The driver swerved and collided with a butcher's boy riding a bike. He fell off sideways and a whole basketful of parcels of meat and sausages fell into the road. The heavy roller blind was stopped in its downward fall by becoming caught on the sidebars just above head height. As quick as I could, I grabbed the pole and pushed its hook back into position to stop it falling any further. None of this carnage was witnessed by any of the staff who I could see through the plate glass windows, putting their coats on and getting ready to leave for the night.

I was shouting at the top of my voice but they couldn't hear me over the traffic and street noise. I now had a gathering group of people who dare not pass under the precarious roller blind and others who were helping the butchers lad, not forgetting the taxi driver who was playing hell behind my back. One man had the wit to rush into the shop and tell them what was going on. I will never forget the look on their faces as they stared out of the window.

The Bunch of Grapes

Jim the pawnbroker asked me to help him shovel some horses manure, which he'd had delivered to his back garden gate. We didn't work on Wednesday afternoons, I never did find out why most shops closed for half a day. Jim and his wife lived in a posh area on the outskirts of Liverpool, in a very nice bungalow. He was a keen gardener who grew all his own vegetables and flowers in an enormous back garden. I had never seen so many healthy looking plants. I was used to seeing things grow from helping Dad in his allotment in Knotty Ash, but this was something else. Everywhere I looked, produce was blooming beautifully, and it was all in neat straight rows and not a weed in sight. It took me about an hour to move the heap of manure with a wheelbarrow to an area near the greenhouse. Jim must have seen me eyeing up the grapes that were growing in his hothouse. "You can have some of those later," he said. This spurred me on to get the job finished. Putting the barrow and spade away, I heard his wife say, "Come and wash your hands Peter". She had prepared a pot of tea and some very nice three corner sandwiches for Jim and me. I felt a bit scared, holding the delicate china cup and saucer and would have been happier with an ordinary plain mug that I was used to. Nevertheless, the sandwiches were delicious; Jim only had one then pushed the plate towards me. When we finished, he took me over to the greenhouse to show me inside. Big bunches of black grapes hung down from the vine over our heads, the vine stretched the full length of the hothouse. He took a pocket-knife and cut a large bunch, which he placed, in a brown paper bag, saying, "Your mother will enjoy these". I noticed the vines roots were in the ground outside the hothouse and had been trained through a hole in the gable end. He took me outside to show me. I asked what sort of fertiliser he used? He replied, "Once a year, I pick up a dead cat from the road and bury it among the roots". He explained, "This gives the plant all the nutrients it needs for a year and the cat gets a decent burial". Back home, we all enjoyed the grapes, they were delicious but I didn't mention Jim's unorthodox fertiliser.

I helped Jim on several occasions after that day, I don't think he and his wife had any children and they became quite fond of me. They made sure I always left with an armful of vegetables, which were very welcome in our household. I was torn between staying at the pawnbrokers, surrounded by nice people and being warm in winter, or going out into the wider world with all its uncertainties. I thought about it for a few weeks until the adventurous side of me took charge; I couldn't visualise growing into manhood as a pawnbroker.

Ale and Hearty

After one and a half years with Hewsons, it was time for me to seek a manlier job than selling crockery and lambswool rugs to old ladies. I started working for a transport firm called James Addey, who had the contract to deliver all the beer for Higsons Brewery. The transport garage was at Beacon Lane, Everton Brow, where all the lorries were parked. Dad and me would walk through to Grant Gardens, West Derby Road in the morning and get the same tram, the 18A. I would get off at Boundary Lane in Everton and he would carry on to Bootle and Seaforth. I was feeling very grown up being on the tram amongst lots of working men, who were dressed in long overcoats and flat caps. Most of them were reading their morning paper and smoking cigarettes and pipes. Like Dad, lots of them were carrying a white enamelled Billycan, which contained a fresh brew of hot tea. The Thermos Flask had either not been invented yet or was not in mass production. In Dad's pocket would be a wrap-up of another brew for later in the day. This consisted of a piece of greaseproof paper with a couple of teaspoons of tealeaves, some sugar and condensed milk dribbled over the top. All it needed was some boiling water. Another funny incident Dad told us about was during the war when he would be working non-stop to unload a ship with his crane. The 'Landing man' on deck signalled him to send down his Billycan. Being so high up, the easiest way was to bring the hook up to his window. Lean out and place the can on the giant hook then send it right down into the ship's hold hundreds of feet below where one of the dockers would take it away to the galley for topping up with boiling water. The driver of the next crane along saw this happening and decided to follow suit. He was a Polish guy and quite new to the job and in bringing up the hook, allowed it to come in towards the window too fast. The massive ball-weight above the hook crashed against the bars in front of the crane's window and bent one of them inwards. Later on that night, a gale blew up and the novice crane driver found he could not close his window due to the bent bar. Dad shouted across to him 'Bring up your hook and put it over the bar, then throw your jib out and winch in very gently, this will straighten the bar back again'. He did all this up to the point of a gentle winch then overdid it. The whole of the front of the crane with all its windows was pulled out and

Mersey Tunnel

went crashing to the ground and ship's deck far below. Within the next thirty minutes, riggers had been up, tied the novice into his seat with rope and fastened up a piece of tarpaulin halfway across the opening. The rain lashed into his cab all night long making him a very miserable soul.

Back to my morning journey, by the time my stop came, the tram would be jam packed full, the windows were all steamed up and you could hear lots of coughing. I was glad to be off and get into the fresh air.

At the garage, I was teamed up with a driver (Stan) and second mate (Jimmy). The lorries were all Albion diesels without starter motors and had to be started by swinging a big brass handle that was sticking out at the front. We would then drive to Upper Parliament Street to the brewery, to load up for the morning's deliveries. Then it was back for a second load for the afternoon. Winter came on with a vengeance in my first year and over the weeks and months, I found my body toughening up with the heavy work and outdoor environment. Although it was hard work, I enjoyed every minute of it, plus the comradeship of ordinary working class men. At home, I would fall fast asleep after the evening meal and Mam would have to wake me up and tell me to go to bed and many times I went to bed without so much as washing my face; I didn't have the energy.

None of the houses had bathrooms, we only had a bath once a week, and that was at the public bathhouse in Balm Street behind Kensington Gardens. Normally, a good stand up scrub was taken at the back kitchen sink. To create a bit more room, Dad had removed the dividing door between the living room and kitchen and replaced it with a sliding door but it was quite noisy whenever it was pushed open or closed. It was also a bit stiff and we had to give it an extra push to get it going. Several weeks later, when Dad had the time, he took the door off and repositioned the rails as well as applying a small amount of Mam's sowing machine oil to the little wheels. None of us were aware of this and each in turn, when we came home, gave the

Liverpool Trams at Pier Head

door the usual hard push. The result was a bang each time it was moved, we had all been conditioned to pushing hard and it was taking some time to recondition ourselves. In the end, Dad said, 'If you keep slamming that door, you'll have it off its hinges'. We all cracked up laughing at the thought of a sliding door having hinges.

I started to get teenage spots all over my face and was persuaded to go and see the head brewer. His office was on the top floor of the brewery and as I climbed the several flights of stairs, I was experiencing a strong smell of ale and my head was becoming dizzy with the fumes. As I reached his office door, I realised the stairs had been alongside an enormous wooden vat, bigger than a ship's funnel, with an open top and I could see a deep layer of foam floating on top of the brew, this was the yeast. The brewer gave me a small brown paper parcel containing live yeast and told me to take a teaspoonful every day and come back if I needed any more. After a couple of weeks, my spots were starting to disappear and my backside became quite sore with the increased visits to the toilet. I never did go back for more yeast.

We were a good team, Stan the driver, Jimmy and I and we got on very well together. Stan had been a lorry driver in the army and had served in Germany. Jimmy had been on this job for about a year, he was the same age as me but his body was as strong as a mans. In cold weather, Fred would put some ether (cold start) into the engines air filter. One of us would take hold of the starting handle and bring the engine to TDC (top dead centre) the driver would wait for our signal and switch on the ignition and slightly press the accelerator. If we were lucky, the engine would start after about six attempts of swinging the handle but in the winter it could take three quarters of an hour to start her up. Then it was all stops out to catch up on the day's work.

In the summer, Jimmy and I would ride on the back of the lorry among the beer barrels and crates during our journeys all around Lancashire and Cheshire. We had good suntans without our shirts on. We were really happy with our lives; I was earning five pounds a week and drinking as much beer as I wanted. I was now putting on weight and had muscles where I never thought I would.

We had lots of funny times. I remember the time that Stan was on holiday and we had a stand-in driver called Harry who smoked a pipe. We were delivering to a pub that had the decorators doing the outside. The decorators had a trestle over the 'Drop', the drop being two big doors in the pavement where we were lowering down the beer. I was on the back of the lorry, passing the crates of beer to Harry who was sliding them down to Jimmy in the cellar. He would catch the crate as it came sliding down the plank and walk off some yards to stack them in the beer cellar. One of the decorators was on the trestle above Harry, burning off the old paint with a blowlamp. Harry was bent over holding a crate on the top of the plank waiting for Jimmy to appear when a piece of burning paint fell onto the back of his neck. Harry let go of the crate, a stream of obscenities came from his mouth as his pipe disappeared down the cellar where Jimmy, who was on his way back, saw the next crate sliding down the plank. He hurtled himself forward to catch it before it hit the floor. Jimmy managed to reach it all right but with the momentum of his added weight, the plank could not take the strain and snapped in two. The top of the plank came forward and smacked Harry under the chin; he was still bent forward trying desperately to remove the hot paint from down his collar. Meanwhile, Jimmy landed in a heap of broken beer bottles and two pieces of broken plank, and wet through with the content., Being a tough young man, he wasn't hurt, but I had a pain that day from laughing.

During my summer holiday when I was just turned seventeen, a few pals and I took a long cycle ride to north Wales. It was the time when cyclists were allowed through the Mersey Tunnel. It was an exhilarating ride, speeding downhill with the traffic and the air current in our favour. We found ourselves whooping with joy, our voices echoing off the walls of the tunnel but our bliss was short lived. At the halfway point, it was all uphill; we found the going very difficult especially when a large lorry came close up behind. I got the feeling we had become a nuisance and we were holding up the progress of the following traffic. I was so glad to see the exit in sight and get out into the fresh air and away from the roar of diesel engines. By lunchtime, we had got to our destination, a tiny village near Mold where we ventured into the only pub for miles around. None of us were at the legal age of drinking but the landlord wasn't going to refuse us, he was obviously thinking of his takings. The tiny pub was very old with bare stone flags and very dark paintwork. Two old men wearing flat caps and both smoking pipes were talking in Welsh. I heard the word 'Liverpool' mentioned a couple of times, they were obviously talking about us but we didn't mind, the beer was starting to have a good effect. Just down the road from the pub, we came across a beautiful orchard of apple trees. I was amazed to see so many big red apples on such small trees, standing there, waiting to be picked. We leaned our bikes against the five-foot fence and used them to climb over. The four of us took separate trees and started stuffing our shirts, the third apple I took hold of wouldn't come off, I gave it a big yank and couldn't believe my eyes, the whole tree lifted up out of the soil. Just then, we heard a shout from the far end of the orchard and scarped back to the fence. I ripped a hole in my skin at waist height in vaulting back over. We were pedalling like mad through the countryside heading for Birkenhead when Frankie Large took a bend too wide and crashed through a hedge. His front wheel buckled so badly, he couldn't ride it. We all sat down to think things through and came up with the idea of stripping his bike down, three of us shared the pieces and Frank would run alongside us on the flat and uphill then sit on someone's crossbar for the downhill stretches. A van towing a flat trailer pulled up and offered us a lift to the tunnel entrance at Birkenhead which we gladly accepted but we decided to use the Ferry for our return over the Mersey as I don't think they would have allowed us to ride through the tunnel carrying extra wheels and a frame with Fankie running alongside.

The Affair

With my new-found wealth, earning over five pounds a week, I decided to buy a new bicycle. I had to take my Mother with me to act as guarantor as I was buying it on the 'never never'. The bike, a Philips Roadster, cost twenty-two pounds and I was in love with it. Over the previous years, I'd had a variety of second hand machines that had been built up from bits and pieces by some back street entrepreneur who sold them for something like ten shillings each. They were always black in colour with sit-up-and-beg handlebars. However, this new one was a bright shiny blue and had drop down handlebars and six gears. After paying mother her board and lodgings, I didn't have much else to do with my money so I soon had it paid off. No more sitting on trams and buses, I was as free as a bird and besides using it for work, I started discovering my home city. At weekends, my cycling took me all over the place, into areas I had become familiar with while on the dray wagons. I was taking a breather in the Bowering Park area one Sunday afternoon and a neighbour from our street came walking past holding on to her husband's arm. 'Hello, fancy seeing you here' I said. 'Oh hello Peter, that's a nice new bike' she replied rather nervously, then went on to tell me that she would be pleased if I didn't mention to anyone that I'd seen her and would I take this five shillings which she quickly put in my hand. I had never seen her husband before that day and was surprised a few weeks later when I saw her real husband painting the front of his house. He looked nothing like the man I'd seen her with in the park but I would never have given it another thought if she hadn't bribed me to keep quiet. I told Mam what had happened, she told Auntie Ann who then told someone else and pretty soon, the whole neighbourhood knew about the affair that was going on between our neighbour a few doors away and some strange man in the park.

War Surplus

Not long after the war, there were several army surplus shops in Liverpool where people could buy all kinds of things. A young man could rig himself out with a complete set of army or airforce clothes for a few shillings. These were ideal for work and it was normal to see people dressed like this every day. One of my brothers was given a military box kite, which he placed on the kitchen table to undo all the straps that were holding it together. It must have been spring-loaded because all of a sudden it expanded into its full size and scattered all the dishes off the table as well as hitting me under the chin. The shop where it came from must have had a job lot as the following evening I saw a much bigger one being flown in Kensington Gardens. The wind had increased quite a lot and the young man holding on to it was being pulled out of the park and along the main road. Everyone stopped to watch as the cord wrapped itself around the overhead tram wires, the aluminium bars of the kite shorted out across the electric cables. There was a massive flash and the kite just disappeared in a ball of flame and smoke. He was left holding a piece of cord with his mouth wide open. Everyone around was laughing his or her heads off.

As I approached the age of eighteen and with an increase in my earnings to seven pounds fifteen shillings a week, I could afford new clothes and ventured into the city on Saturday nights with my mate Billy Thompson. We were two young lads and very unsophisticated in the art of drinking in pubs. In the Legs of Man pub on the corner of Lime Street, Billy was just about to pick up his pint when a huge hand got there before him. The owner of the hand was an equally huge man, and the pint glass at his lips was emptying very quickly through a mouth that didn't seem to have a gullet. "That's my beer" said my mate, but the giant kept drinking, then putting the empty glass on the bar, leaned forward and in a very quiet voice replied "Whose friggin beer?" "Ok, I guess its yours", said Billy. The Legs of Man was off our list from that moment on.

If the truth was known, I was always glad when Monday mornings came around again, I seemed to get more pleasure during my working hours than getting all dressed up just to stand around in pubs and waste good money getting drunk.

Higsons Brewery had a department for making beer barrels and we all witnessed a young cooper who had completed his apprenticeship one-day. The tradition for this particular trade is being put inside the last barrel he has made and having wet hops and ale thrown in on top of him and being rolled around the brewery yard a few times to the cheers of everyone there.

There were lots of incidents involving brewery deliveries and looking back, it was one of the best jobs I'd had but time marches on and my next adventure was being employed by the country's biggest firm, Her Majesty's Armed Forces.

Call Up

Young men of a certain age (eighteen) had to listen to the radio for an announcement telling them that they should report to the Ministry of Labour and register for National Service.

For eighteen years, I was known, called and recognised, as Peter. I was happy enough with the name, unlike several friends of mine, especially girls, who hated their given names. I think Peter is quite a good name, it reminds one of St. Peter or Salt Peter or Peter Pan. What other name would I want? Anyway, I was satisfied with it and grew up without giving it much thought. That was, until the day I got called up to serve my Queen and Country. I had just turned eighteen and was about to register at the employment office, just like the man on the radio told me. "All young men, born between February the 1st 1938 and March the 1st 1938 should report to their local labour exchange to register for National Service." Mother searched in her box of family documents for my birth certificate, which was needed for entry into the Forces. "Who is this Shaun, Mam?" I asked, "You've given me the wrong one." (There were eight kids in our family) "Oh, I'd forgotten about that" she said, and then explained. "It is your certificate, Aunt Agnes took you to be registered as a baby and came back with a certificate showing you as Shaun." She went on to say, "I told her, I wanted you named Peter but she had to have her own way. I took you back the next day and asked the registrar to change the document but he told me, he couldn't do that, as it was an official certificate, which couldn't be altered. But he did say, he could just squeeze in the name Peter after Shaun, he also said, "You call him Peter, it won't make any difference" so I did and forgot all about it until now."

Author back row, third from left

I couldn't wait to go in the Forces and in no time I was having my medical at the army selection office in Moorfields. On arriving home with a beaming smile and my declaration showing me A.1. fit and healthy I told my mother that I had signed on as a regular for twenty-two years. "My God" she said, "what have you done that for?"

I told her that as a national serviceman, my pay would have been only three shillings a day but by signing on as a regular and with the option of leaving after three years, my pay is going to be seven shillings a day. Therefore, "I will be able to send you more money home." She grabbed me and gave me a big hug. When Dad came home, he too was very proud that his third son was going to be a serviceman. My big brother Bryan had not long come back from Hong Kong where he'd been for two years with the Army and Gerald, my next eldest brother was still in the Royal Navy, serving on Aircraft Carriers. My younger brother Chris, who was still a young boy would also follow in the family tradition and join the Army as a regular soldier before the age of eighteen.

The service life was not going to be a shock to me as I had been in both the Airforce and Army cadets. At the age of thirteen, I went to summer camp as an air cadet and had flown twice in a Tiger Moth, the two seated, open cockpit bi-plane. These planes were from the First World War and were covered in canvas. They could take off from grass in about half the length of a football field.

During the final two weeks before leaving Liverpool and heading for my big adventure, Billy Thompson, one of my mates did everything to try and persuade me to change my mind but I was having none of it. On the last evening, we had 'a bit of a do' in our local, The Royal Arch in Kensington. Two local girls, who we didn't know very well, Joyce and Betty, decided to accompany Billy and me down to Lime Street Station. They had edged their way into our little get-together in the pub and had been hitting the gin and orange a bit too much. Joyce was all over me like a rash, drawling her words out. My train was leaving at midnight and as I stood onboard with my head out of the carriage window, I was having a job getting her hands from around my neck as the train was pulling away. She had tears streaming down her cheeks leaving streaks of mascara; I could hear her high heels moving faster and faster along the platform.

'Let go' I shouted, thinking she was going to get dragged under the train. Billy and the other girl were running along behind her, he managed to grab her around the waist at the very last minute and they both bowled head over heels on the platform. They seemed ok as they stood up, waving frantically I waved back as the train disappeared around a bend then took my seat.

I never gave my send off another thought because I was too busy contemplating my future. The compartment I was in had no other occupants and I was able to stretch out along the plushly upholstered seats. My thoughts went back to the interview I'd had with the recruiting officer and my choice of going into a Corps rather than an Infantry Regiment. My idea was to acquire some sort of skill that would benefit me when I came out of the Army. I signed up with the Royal Army Service Corps where I knew I would be taught to drive. Being a regular soldier, I would be able to go on a specialist course of my choice so I opted for the Fire Service. The train came to a halt at Crewe Station, I could hear doors slamming, and a whistle blowing, then we were off again. Before long, the door to my compartment opened, a ticket inspector asked to see my ticket. I was informed that I was in a first class compartment and I only had a third class ticket. No wonder I was the only occupant! Twenty minutes later, after searching every third class carriage in the train, I still hadn't found a vacant seat and had to spend the remainder of the journey sitting in the corner of a draughty corridor.

In defence of the Realm

Blenheim Barracks, Aldershot, was almost deserted when I arrived. It was the Friday afternoon before August bank holiday and it seemed that everyone except a handful of staff had been given leave. The recruiting sergeant in Liverpool had made an error with my reporting date. It should have been the Friday

81

before. As a result of his incompetence, I had missed the intake for the training camp in Somerset and had to spend the next five weeks in Aldershot waiting for the following course. With the quartermasters stores being closed, I could not get kitted out until the following Tuesday. Five days wearing the same clothes, and because the bedding stores were closed also, I had to sleep in a bed without sheets and I was lucky to find that bed in the only billet in the camp with occupants; three guys who had no families to go home to. By the time Tuesday came, I was looking a mess; I had washed my one and only shirt, socks and underwear during the weekend and managed to get them dry in the hot August sunshine. The only saving grace was the food. Three good meals a day and supper if we were still hungry. There's one good thing about the forces; they never let their servicemen go hungry. When the quartermaster's stores finally opened on the Tuesday morning, I was fully kitted out with everything from top to bottom. I couldn't wait to discard my now grubby suit and get into some new khaki. They gave us some brown paper and string to wrap up our civilian clothes to send home, I put mine into the nearest dustbin.

My five weeks in Aldershot were spent doing guard duties, fire pickets and kitchen fatigues. All the time, I was seething at the thought of missing out on the previous intake due to some beer bellied NCO who was probably finishing his last few years in the army, behind a recruiting desk and giving very little thought or enthusiasm to the job in hand. It was during this period of my life that I cultivated antipathy towards incompetent people in positions of authority. They reminded me too much of my old school teacher who didn't give a damn about his work as long as the salary kept being paid.

I came into the billet one day to see a chap from Manchester doing something unusual. He had a wet towel wrapped around his knee and was belting it with the back of a tablespoon. He was a national service man who was trying to get a medical discharge by giving himself 'Water on the Knee'. A few days later, a big black lad from London was hoping to get a discharge because every time he shaved, his face bled profusely. He told me quietly, he'd started by rubbing a new razor blade on the concrete path before shaving. His face was in a terrible mess and I'm sure he would have been scarred for life. They just didn't want anything to do with the forces and were putting themselves through these bizarre actions to get out of army life. I personally couldn't understand their logic; they would probably end up in some factory or building site and be bored to tears with their existence. At the end of five weeks, I was transferred with about 50 other guys to our training camp, Blenhiem Barracks near Yeovil, Somerset where we met our instructors face to face. In the first week, they did their best to break us down and drive every last vestige of civilian life out of our brains. The training corporals were the worst, they thought they were little Gods because they had so much power and control over us. Some young men couldn't take it and absconded. The official term is A.W.O.L, Absent Without leave.

I accepted all the discipline thrown at me and sailed through my basic training with ease. This was the first time I could understand what I was supposed to learn. The teachers and instructors were brilliant; I devoured every piece of information and instruction given. I wouldn't go to bed at night without spending some time on revision and getting my kit ready for the following day. Every Saturday morning, we had a big parade were the RSM would inspect our turn out. My battle dress would be pressed to perfection, a skill I had learned as a Cadet. Some guys in the billet asked me to press theirs and offered to pay me two shillings each. Friday nights saw me still up after midnight pressing a dozen uniforms while all around, having spent the evening in the NAAFI were now fast asleep but when pay day came, I was on the receiving end of quite a bit of money. We went through all the soldiering stuff, like charging at stuffed dummies with fixed bayonets while screaming our heads off and splashing about in muddy water on the assault course. For those of us still on the cadre after six weeks and the mummies boys had been back squadded, driver training started. This is what I'd been looking forward to. We were given less than fifteen hours to learn how to drive a three-ton truck and pass the test. I did mine in twelve. Our driving instructors were all civilians and Mr Prince who taught me was one of the nicest people I had ever come across. His teaching method enabled me to pass my test in a very short time. One afternoon while driving through the beautiful Somerset countryside, he asked me to pull up in front of his house, which was a whitewashed thatched cottage. His wife asked me to get some fresh water from the well in her garden and I remember being fascinated at winding the handle that brought the bucketful of clean fresh water to the top. After our cup of tea, we headed back for the camp. I passed the driving test without difficulty and received the little red book to show I was a competent driver. Further driver training consisted of a couple of days learning how to keep the truck going after a theoretical wheel had been blown off by a landmine or stuffing a flat tyre with grass to keep it on the road. Then came a spell of learning to tow each other and night driving. I was behind the wheel of truck number sixteen in a line of twenty-five heading out of camp on a cold winters' night. It was exhilarating, having nobody beside me for the first time. One thing that we were not given enough instruction on, was convoy tactics. We learned this at a later stage in our army career. This was the stratagem of closing up the convoy in built up areas and keep moving regardless of traffic lights and stop signs. This only works if the lead vehicle keeps to a sensible speed and everyone else keeps in close formation. This manoeuvre will not be found in any military training manual, as it means breaking the rules of the Highway Code. I have been in convoys in Asia and Europe using this method with great results. The convoys never got split up, never took the wrong route and always arrived on time. What civilian driver, would dare to try and get in among a line of big army trucks with gaps not big enough to get a Mini in between them? Even the police used to stop while our convoys went through red lights.

Our night convoy of novice drivers with the exception of the leader started spreading out as a mist came down all around the Somerset countryside. The inevitable happened when number four lost sight of truck number three and took the wrong fork. The result was, twenty-two three-ton trucks ended up in the driveway of a large country house with not enough room to turn around. We all gained a lot of reversing experience that night.

Our passing out parade was a big success. We marched to the sound of a military band and felt very proud with our achievements. Lots of parents and families came to see their sons during and after the parade. My parents could ill afford the journey down from Liverpool and I never mentioned it to them. Most of the new drivers were posted to transport companies in West Germany, Scotland or Wales. One or two went to Malta and Cyprus. Twenty-six of us went on a specialist course to the civilian Fire Headquarters Training School in Guildford, Surrey. For the next five weeks, we trained hard and learned every aspect of firefighting, including the now banned, hook ladder drill. I understand that the fire-fighters union had it taken out of service because it was considered too dangerous to use. This particular piece of equipment was in the shape of a wooden ladder, thirteen feet long, with a hinged metal hook at one end. It was for use in places where there was no access for a turntable escape. In use, the fireman would lift the ladder up over his head towards the second floor of a burning building. Smash the hook through the window and climb the ladder. When he got to the window, he would use his axe to smash out the window and centre frame so he could get his leg over the sill and sit on the window ledge while pulling the ladder up and past him towards the third floor. If the fire were further up the building, he would repeat this operation from floor to floor. Each time the axe was used, there was the danger of falling glass but this was nothing compared to the danger of the hook becoming dislodged. In training, we only went to the third floor and even this felt extremely high. The key to using the ladder correctly was to keep your arms at full stretch in the ascent and descent. This caused our feet to push the ladder tighter into the wall, thus keeping it stable. One or two trainees became a bit frightened and pulled their body close to the ladder, this caused it to start swinging like a pendulum. The instructor below would shout out a command and the trainee reluctantly straightened his arms. None of us enjoyed this bit of training but we all managed to complete the drill. I am not surprised at the trade unions decision to have the ladder taken out of service; not everyone is a Spiderman.

Although we had civilian instructors, we worked and trained separately from the civilian trainees. Our course curriculum was the same as theirs but four weeks shorter as we already knew how to stand to attention etc. This was the second period of training that I thoroughly enjoyed. What a difference when the teachers are competent, interested in every pupil and make you feel like you're achieving something. The truck took us back to the accommodation block somewhere in Guildford for the last time. We paraded in front of our commanding officer to hear our results and postings.

My dream came true; I was being posted to Singapore. My big brother Bryan had done his National service in Hong Kong, I remember the excitement I felt as a twelve-year-old when reading the letters he sent home from the Far East. Now it was my turn - I was going Singapore in Asia, wherever that was, and I would be away from home for the next two and a half years. I couldn't wait.

Fraudulent Members of the Cavern Club

In less than an hour, my kit was packed and I was on a train heading for Liverpool and four weeks pre-embarkation leave with loads of money in my pocket, most of it earned from my ironing jobs. The weeks dragged, I wanted to be away, around the other side of the world, and instead I was going out to smoky pubs, pretending to enjoy myself. Billy and I did go to the Cavern Club in Mathew street a few times. We weren't members but in a pub nearby, we would take the cork lining out of a beer bottle top and use it to fasten the top (we called them Jinks) to our shirt. In the gloomy entrance of the Cavern, we would flick open our jacket lapel to show quick flash of our fake club badge. I think it was the top off Bass's Red Label beer bottle that was closest to the club's badge design. We always got in without paying. Cilla Black the television presenter and singer worked there as a girl in the cloakroom, her real name was Pricilla White and her Dad worked on the docks. The Cavern was a Jazz club but every week they had guest groups in to play modern stuff like Rock and Roll, especially in the afternoons. One group of longhaired young men were becoming quite a hit with the girls and the acoustics of the Cavern were ideal for their howling but the acoustics were much better for the Jazz musicians whom we went to listen to. The Jazzmen's instruments were all battered and bent but this didn't seem to have any effect on their music, they sounded brilliant. The Beatles went on to become very famous but personally, I didn't think much of them. If it hadn't been for the 'Teeny Boppers' (young teenage girls) screaming their heads off I don't think they'd have got far.

Finally, my four weeks leave came to an end. I said my goodbyes to my parents, grandparents, Ssiblings, and neighbours. My mates and a bevy of girls escorted me to Lime Street Station once again. After lots of hugs and kisses, they all promised to write; one or two kept their promise.

I was in full uniform and had all my kit with me on my journey to the transit camp.

The train journey was quite pleasant because I was in a carriage surrounded by three young women who were going down to Plymouth. They had all joined the Royal Navy and were about to embark on their basic training. They wanted to know what I had experienced in my training and I suddenly felt very mature in being able to advise them what I knew about service life and what training I had already gone through.

One of the girls asked me if I would write to her but none of us knew exactly where we were going or our forwarding addresses. It would have been impossible to try and keep in touch with me going halfway around the world.

Army Wives Exposed

I arrived at our battalion transit camp in Borden, Hampshire where hundreds of us gathered to spend another five weeks waiting for a troopship. There are only so many duties than can be carried out in any camp, guarding the place, cleaning, fire pickets, or cookhouse fatigues but I did get a job of driving a two ton truck for a couple of weeks. Delivering small tin baths full of coal to the married quarters. I was glad when it came to an end as my blushes were in danger of becoming a permanent feature from being greeted at the door by scantily clad women. To stop us from being bored, our kit had to be pressed and folded in flat squares of nine inches by nine. Their reason being, that if we were to leave in a hurry, it would be quicker to pack our kit bags! This being a transit camp and not a training camp, no foot drill was carried out with the exception of parading. We paraded almost every day, sometimes three times a day, all this was to take time up and shorten the hours of boredom. Most of us longed to see our names on a duty roster just to get out of parading. Saturday morning parades were the worst; there was a big inspection of the barrack blocks and ourselves by the Commanding Officer who was accompanied by the Regimental Sergeant Major. It was winter and we would be dressed in our Greatcoats that were buttoned up to our necks. Some months previously while in training camp, I had overcome the problem of 'dangling brass buttons' by the use of an "old soldiers" trick. By cutting all the front buttons off, making small incisions in the coat, pushing the metal back loop, through the material and threading a leather bootlace on the inside of the coat and through all the button loops. When the coat was worn, the two rows of large brass buttons looked perfectly flush and immaculate, they were also easier to remove and clean than having them sown onto the material.

The guy in the next bed saw what I had done and did the same to his coat. However, on parade morning, the RSM noticed one of his buttons upside down and took hold to twist it straight. I was only two positions from him and watched as the RSM had difficulty straightening the button up and started to pull, one by one, the buttons popped off and fell to the parade ground as the leather bootlace slid out of their loops. The RSMs face was livid as the charade unfolded. He screamed at the soldier saying, "You will be charged for defacing her Majesty's property and you will be made to pay for a new Greatcoat now get off my parade ground left-right-left-right".

Finally, we got the order to move. Our journey to Southampton was on an old steam train nicknamed "The Borden Bullet".

We had a nice journey through the Hampshire countryside, across southern England and down to the south coast. The train went right into the dockside sheds where we alighted with all our kit. We had previously stencilled our large kitbags with our name, rank, regiment and number. They were piled onto a cargo sling and hoisted up over the ship's rail and stowed somewhere in the hold of Her Majesty's Troopship, *Nevasa*. We had been ordered to pack only the necessary items of kit needed for the voyage into our webbing packs, which we would keep on board. There seemed to be thousands of troops from many different regiments gathering on the quayside. There were lots of transit staff with armbands and military police to herd us up and guide us to the correct gangplank. Our sleeping quarters (troop-deck) was very crammed when everybody was in, trying to pack their kit away into small lockers and sorting our beds which were three tiers high. That done, we assembled on the upper decks to watch the ship being untied and gently moving away from the quayside where her Majesty's Royal Marines Commandos Regimental band were playing *'Land of Hope and Glory'*. Hundreds of people waved us off, shaking their handkerchiefs. It was a very moving and emotional experience for all of us and I loved every minute of it especially when an instruction came over the ship's tannoys to raise our hats and give three cheers to Great Britain. The noise of everyone on board and the ship's horns blasting out over the town of Southampton was fantastic. I thought, 'This is it, I'm off on an adventure of a lifetime and it would be over two and a half years before I would see my homeland again.' My excitement was only marred once during the five week voyage as we crossed the Bay of Biscay, that notorious stretch of the Atlantic between France and Spain. It was early February when we hit a force seven gale. After breakfast on the second morning, my head started spinning, my mouth went dry but fluid was rising up in my throat. It was a most horrible feeling, which I'd never, experienced before. Someone said, 'You've got seasickness'. Anyone who doesn't get sick at sea should consider himself or herself very fortunate. It's a most horrible experience and I felt as though I wanted to die. We had been ordered to stay below decks during the bad weather, but life on the troop decks was pretty nauseous, with so many of us cramped up, there's always the odd dirty sod who has smelly feet.

I had to find my own cure and it was outside in the fresh air. After muster and roll call each morning, I would sneak away and make my way up onto a deserted part of the ship that I found by climbing over a gate marked 'Crew Only'. After another two flights of steps, I discovered a small sheltered area above the Captains Bridge where I spent many happy hours each day. I would watch the ship's progress through the storm, the bow rising up on giant waves then crashing down into deep troughs where millions of gallons of seawater would cascade over the front of the ship. After an hour of sea watching, I would get my nose into a good book which made the time fly by. At lunchtime, I'd have my snack, which had been discreetly pocketed during breakfast and continued with my sea watching and reading until it was time for the evening meal. The ship was such a big place and it was easy to disappear for hours at a time without being missed. On the fourth day, my luck ran out, I had been discovered and ordered to return below decks but the weather had started to settle down and we were heading in towards Las Palmas in the Canary Islands to take on fresh water. This was my first foreign visit and I can remember almost every detail. The sun was shining out of a beautiful blue sky, the temperature was like a hot summer's day in Britain and we were wearing the shorts of our tropical kit for the first time. On board, they told us we had just three hours shore leave and anyone not back onboard by 2pm would be left behind. My pal Ginger and I went for a long walk around the small coastal town. The houses were all painted white, little old ladies dressed in black, sat on rickety old chairs outside their front doors crocheting what looked like small white table cloths. The cobbled streets were all narrow and old men led donkeys slowly along, they were loaded with firewood or sacks of something unknown. A funeral cortege was in progress outside a large church. The priest with a tall crucifix in his hands led the coffin being carried by four men, a stream of mourners following behind. Some of the mourners carried big bunches of white lilies. It was all very solemn looking and judging by the ages of the people in attendance, the deceased must have been someone old. Further down the same street, we passed a noisy bar with a beaded curtain over the doorway. As we walked past it smelled strongly of tobacco and stale beer, we could hear a male foreign language being spoken inside, I guessed it must have been Spanish. This strange tongue was a complete new experience for me and which I thought sounded pleasant. A little shop next door with the word Tabac over the door had a selection of smoker's requisites in the window. Apart from the church, the tallest and newest building we saw, was back near the port where the ship was berthed. It looked like a hotel, about four storeys high. Opposite was a beach where people sunbathed, they looked like holidaymakers. Strong surf was washing up on the beach with one or two hardy swimmers being tossed about in the waves. It looked very inviting and we wished we had more time and our swimming trunks with us.

Campagnia

Our long route to the Far East, around the Cape of South Africa came around as a result of the Middle East War or The Suez Crisis as it was called. On the 29th of October 1956, Colonel Gamal Abdel Nasser, the president of Egypt had decided to illegally nationalise the Anglo French Canal Company. While the British Prime Minister, Anthony Eden, was deciding what to do about it, the Israeli military forces invaded. The Brits and French followed suit a few days later but had to withdraw after only a couple of days when the USA, USSR and United Nations condemned their action. The Suez Canal was blocked when a lot of ships were sunk during the fighting causing all shipping to make the much longer journey around South Africa for the next couple of years.

I was still in Aldershot when this happened and was behind the counter in the Quartermasters Stores, issuing kit to the 'Z' reservists who had been called up. It all had to be done quickly, there was no time to measure men up, and they were told to sort themselves out outside. It was comical to see them in their underwear, a short fat man holding a pair of pants against himself that would have fitted a six footer, then swapping them with someone else who had just the opposite. The reservists were all drivers of the RASC. They had to be issued with Sten Guns, a short barrelled machine gun. We had spent the whole of the previous day preparing these weapons. They had been stored in pieces, wrapped in waterproof paper that was covered in grease. By the end of the day, we had all become experts at assembling the Sten Gun. New trucks painted in desert camouflage were rolling up and being signed over to the Z-Men. When enough were assembled, they would set off in convoy down to the south coast where they would be shipped out to the Middle East. It was quite an exciting few days for me, to be involved in a massively organised military event such as this.

Our next port of call was Durban on the east coast of Africa where we had shore leave. As ours was only the second British troop-ship to call there since the Second World War, it caused quite a stir among the British settlers living in and around Durban. They thronged the quayside, waiting for us as we came down the gangplank. Guys were being bungled into limousines and whisked off to be given VIP treatment for a couple of hours at their farms and plantations. These ex-pats were hungry for news on a personal level from the homeland. By the time my mates and I got off the ship, all the limousines had gone. We wanted to see the city so went for a walk. It was a real eye-opener to see this beautiful city with its wide-open spaces, fountains and majestic buildings. The big Zulu men, who pulled the taxi rickshaws in bare feet with soles like leather, amazed us. They had tall plumes of colourful feathers above their heads and anklets of bells round their legs. It was a colourful and spectacular sight to see one passing us at high speed, going downhill with two passengers in the back. We stood and watched with our mouths open as the giant barefoot warrior, like a horse between the shafts of a cart, suddenly jumped up, the carriage tilted backwards but couldn't go any further as it had a jockey wheel at the rear. The Zulu's legs were pedalling in mid air as the carriage continued its freewheeling downhill journey and the driver singing what sounded like a tribal war song, fading into the distance.

We sauntered a bit too far, and found ourselves in the seedy quarter of Durban, only realising something was just not right by the amount of eyes staring at us. We were the only white skinned people among hundreds of blacks and we were in military uniform. Being as casual as we could, we stopped to look at some goods in a shop window, then slowly retraced our steps until we came across an old English looking pub in the European district. The barman said, 'You probably would have been alright, but I would never go there'.

Back on the quayside, a fruit seller had set up his stall; I bought a whole stalk of about forty bananas for a shilling. They were for my mates on board who couldn't get shore leave because some people were needed to carry out duties such as fire pickets etc. At the top of the gangplank, one of the ships officers warned me there might be a poisonous spider lurking in the bunch, which I was carrying on my shoulder. I don't know why I wasn't worried, maybe it was the two glasses of rum we'd had in the bar which cost three pence a tot and the tots were something like a quarter of a pint. South Africa produces a lot of Rum from all the sugar cane they grow there.

Unforgettable Memories

The journey across the Indian Ocean was something that will stay in my memory forever. The sea was so calm, like an enormous millpond, like a sheet of glass that went on for miles and miles, for days and days. The heat was affecting us all now and below decks it was stifling. It was the first time we were allowed to open the portholes on our troop-deck down near the waterline. Lots of us slept on the open decks with just a pillow and sheet. The dawns and sunsets where fantastic as we watched the sun either rising or dropping out of sight on the horizon, creating a beam of golden light twenty-five miles long on the surface of the sea. One day there was a buzz of excitement when thousands of sea snakes were seen all around the ship, just below the surface. Most days we witnessed flying fish taking off in front of the ship and flapping their big fins, which looked like transparent wings. They could fly just above the sea's surface for hundreds of metres. Another delightful spectacle were the dolphins that swam for hours close to the bow wave, as though they were playing and really enjoying themselves. One afternoon, I was lying on my top bunk, reading the novel, Swiss Family Robinson. Without noticing, the ship went gently into a slow roll as we started moving into different waters. I was brought back to reality from the story I was engrossed in by a sudden shout of alarm. The light in the troop-deck suddenly changed. Twisting my head to the left, I was amazed to see five giant spouts of seawater coming in through the open portholes. The sun's rays were being deflected through the water, like beautiful prisms turning the whole of our troopdeck into a brilliant shade of turquoise. As the ship gently rolled back, several guys nearest to them dashed through two feet of seawater to close and fasten the portholes. Our troopdeck was only about two to three metres above sea level and the ship didn't take much tilting for our portholes to be under water. Automatic klaxon bells started clanging and the big steel doors at the bottom of the steps began to close, shutting off our only escape route. To a man, we made one almighty dash for the stairway, fortunately there were only about twenty of us below decks that afternoon and we all managed to get out before the door slammed shut. By the time we could go back down, the pumps had removed all the water and it was almost dry.

Our next port of call was Colombo on the Island of Ceylon (now Sri Lanka) it was my turn to be fire picket and remain on board. The only experience I had of that questionably exotic place was from others who told me of their sights, sounds and smells when they returned from their visit. Apparently it was very dirty, very smelly and none said they would like to go back again. The highlight of their visit was the many elephants with pink ears they'd seen.

I was wondering how much of the local brew they'd had to drink until someone informed me that Indian Elephants do have a pink tinge towards the edges of their ears and they are smaller than the African Elephant.

Journey to the unknown

The ship had left Southampton on 2nd February and we were pulling into Singapore on the 4th of March 1957. The weather was now seriously hot, being just two degrees off the equator. Reunited with our kitbags, we were shown to some corrugated tin huts that were no more than sunshades in reality and told to get some rest. We were shown a standpipe outside with a tap at the top and told to use it if we got thirsty. One or two of us tried and you could have made tea with the water, it was so hot. There were iron-sprung beds in the huts but no mattresses. The walls had gaps both top and bottom. The floor was bare earth and there was no door. Just as we were wondering what sort of camp they had brought us to and how we were going to spend the night, we were herded off to a large store and in turn, made to sign for a rifle and ammunition. Then we were loaded onto trucks and taken to Singapore railway station where a sleeper train was waiting for us. Inside the concourse high above our heads was an enormous Mosaic Mural, depicting the building of the notorious Japanese railway by prisoners of war. It showed emaciated allied troops toiling on the track in the fierce heat while figures of Japanese guards stood over them with large bamboo canes and in threatening postures; it was a scene of pure misery.

During the Second World War, Singapore fell to a Japanese invasion. Lt General Arthur Percival led the surrender of the largest amount of British led forces in history. The Japanese invaders took prisoner, 33,000 British and 17,000 Australian forces. Most of them were put to work on the railway and 16,000 allied prisoners of war died through disease, illness and starvation.

[On Friday 13th February 1942, The Japanese Army went through Alexander Hospital in Singapore, bayoneting doctors, nurses, and even patients on operating tables. Altogether, there were over 2,000 allied forces and patients killed in and around the hospital in one day.]

The carriages of our train were similar to those of the American Wild West, with open platforms each end. Two soldiers stood on each platform, manning machine guns that were mounted on brackets. At the front of the train, were a separate engine and wagon that were heavily armour plated. A big searchlight was mounted on the front and several canons were pointing out in all directions. This separate unit was to leave ten minutes before the main train to make sure the track was clear from ambush. The Army Catering Corps had supplied us with a meal and some haversack rations on the platform. I was soon settling down in my bunk bed. As the train gathered speed I was looking out of the window at the night sky and thick jungle and was feeling a little apprehensive. Originally, my posting

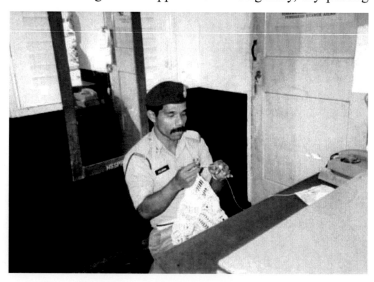

A Malayan solider doing his crocheting

had been to Singapore, that beautiful island at the southern tip of Malaya, and then just three days ago, we had been given a lecture onboard about the Communist Terrorists in Malaya.

Apparently, during the Second World War and after the Japanese occupation, we the British had employed the use of a guerrilla force of locals to carry out counter espionage work against the enemy, with a promise of independence after the war. We, the British, did not keep our promise so they turned their aggression towards us. Eleven years later, we were still fighting them. This was a scarcely known war back home and the British War Office chose to call it an emergency instead. Consequently, there was very little news published in the British press. Few people coming out to Malaya on our troopship and at home were aware that we were going into a war zone. Now, we were on a heavily armed train, heading somewhere up north, through the ULU (Jungle).

I couldn't sleep for ages and lay staring out of the window. My imagination was running wild at the thought of hundreds of Chinese Terrorists watching the train, getting ready to pounce any minute or laying a massive ambush miles from anywhere. I heard several guys loading their magazines behind their curtains so I was not alone with my thoughts. I did the same and kept my rifle very close.

Tiredness eventually took over and I slept soundly, the noise of the train wheels clicking over the joints in the track had a very soothing and hypnotic effect. It's amazing how the dawn changes one's perspective, we were all feeling in a buoyant mood as the train pulled into a small station somewhere along the single track. With rifles slung over our backs, we stood in line on the platform in bright sunshine, waiting for our breakfast which had been laid on once again by the Catering Corps who must have come from some nearby camp. Later that day, on our journey north, groups of men were leaving the train at various stopping places up country; eventually after many hours it was our turn to alight. That is, Ginger Hickman, a national serviceman and myself. We had been on the same Fire Course in Guildford and had been posted to a place called 'Teiping'. Well, it must have been a typing error by some clerk because they weren't expecting us and knew nothing about our posting to their camp. A few hours later and after several signals, (the forces did all their communication by radio signal, using Morse Code) we found where we should have gone. As it was too late to leave, we were given meals and beds. My first experience of the tropics in that small camp made a pleasant assault on my senses as I lay back on the bed, listening to the cicadas and crickets singing in the trees, feeling the warmth of the night air while under the mosquito net and catching the feint aroma of spicy foods, drifting in from somewhere outside. How different all this is from the back streets of Liverpool I thought. What would Mam and Dad be doing right now? It is the beginning of March, they would be sitting in front of the fire, and it would probably be raining. The following morning, we were put on the southbound train heading back down the track. A hundred miles later, we alighted at Tapah Road and found there was no military vehicle waiting for us, as they weren't expecting anyone off the southbound train. The train we just left was full of troops from up near the Siam (Thailand) border who were on their way to the United Kingdom and would be going back home, on the same ship that had brought us to the Far East on its return from Hong Kong.

Through enemy lines by bus

I made enquiries with the stationmaster, a tall Sikh gentleman with a blue turban on his head. He spoke perfect English and replied, "The only way you will get to your camp is on that bus" and he hastened us to get on it quickly, as it was about to leave. We paid the fare and the driver showed us to the back seats where we were able to spread out, having so much kit and weapons. We stopped in the local town to fill up with more passengers and a whole array of goods, which we could see being loaded onto the long roof rack. These included some live pigs and chickens in baskets. We set off on a forty-seven mile journey up the mountains. The sounds, sights and aromas on the bus were all strange to us. Several people were eating food from the three or four tier aluminium containers they were carrying. These were clever devices comprising of what looked like small saucepans with lids stacked one on top of the other and kept together with a leather strap and carrying handle. When opened, the food smelled delicious and spicy. I was watching a woman in a seat forward of us, she had a type of Chapatti bread in the top container, a delicious smelling curry in the one underneath and some fresh fruit in the lower one. None of them had cutlery, they were using their fingers, ever so gently.

Ginger and I were feeling very hungry as we hadn't had a bite since breakfast and the Teiping camp hadn't thought to give us haversack rations. The bus made calls at various tiny hillside villages on the way up the mountain. At what I guessed was the halfway point, everyone got off but the driver put his hand up to us and beckoned us to stay on board. Through the windows, we could see people buying bottles of orange juice etc., the bus driver came on board with two bottles for us but wouldn't take any money. I could only think that he'd got them free for bringing a lot of customers to the shop. I don't remember how many hours the journey took but it was dark when the driver indicated that we had reached our destination. The small camp (Station Lines) was the first assembly of buildings you come to at the six thousand feet level. The whole range of the Cameron Highlands was covered in thick tropical rain forest and the camp was created out of a small clearing. There were about a dozen munitions type huts with corrugated roofs. Detachments of RASC were stationed there with a fleet of four-ton Bedford trucks. There was a smaller detachment of Australian Service Corps with just three American type GMC trucks. A detachment of the Kings Dragoon Guards with Ferret scout cars, a small REME (Royal Electrical and Mechanical Engineers) workshop and the fire-fighting unit where we were going to work. There was just one cook with a local boy to look after our needs and of course, the NAAFI. Total manpower was about thirty-five men. The Transport Company would be taking goods and fighting troops under escort up and down the mountain six days a week, leaving the camp very short staffed. If the Commies had known this, we could have given very little opposition in a sustained attack on the camp. It was to be my home for the next nineteen months, the place where I grew up, the place where I became a man. We walked down the slope towards the main gate and got a most unusual look from the sentry on duty.

Ginger and I stood in the company office, two pale faced 'Sprogs from Blighty'. The C.O., was amazed by our unconventional arrival. The sergeant major next to him bellowed, "You came on a public bus? Don't you realise that we have to move up and down that road in convoy, escorted by armoured cars and you two came up on a f***ing bus?" We were the talk of the Highlands for days after and we realised why the bus driver didn't want us to get off at the halfway stop.

Introduction to Malaya

Our main job was to provide fire cover for the many helicopter sorties that took place. Fighting troops would be airlifted to and from the nearest football field (Padang) at Tanah Rata to outlying jungle stations called 'Forts' and our secondary roll was to provide fire cover for several other military establishments and the many civilians who were living in the mountains.

The weather was very inclement at that altitude; it was the only place in the tropics where we were issued with four blankets. When it wasn't raining, the climate was very like an English summer, which is one reason why so much farming was done in the highlands. Many kinds of fruit and vegetables were grown including strawberries; they became a favourite delicacy of mine and still are.

Malaya is a peninsular of land hanging off what is now known as Thailand. It was a British Colony with mining and plantation interests. The country was divided up into states and Straits Settlements, each with its own ruler, a Sultan. The states comprised of Singapore, Penang, Wellesley and Malacca. The Federated Malay states (FMS) of Perak, Selangor, Negri-Sembilan, Pehang, Johore, Kedah, Kelantan and Perlis. Each state had its own currency, which was used throughout the country. The Prime Minister at that time was Tunku Abdul Rahman.

We were stationed in Pehang, the largest state, that was famous for its population of tigers. The beautiful Bengal tiger was depicted on most banknotes and postage stamps. I came across one while driving a Landrover one evening; it ran across my path and bounded up a steep escarpment. I just happened to drive past that spot the next morning and stopped to show two others who were with me. The tiger left its claw prints in the clay of the embankment and they were enormous, much larger than we could spread our own hands.

It made us all realise just how big some of these creatures were. The most dangerous things we had to be aware of was malaria and dengue fever. More people are killed world-wide from Malaria than any other cause. Up in the mountains, there was little concern about malaria, as the mosquito could not survive the cooler climate. However, if we went down to the low lands we had to take strict precautions every day. Each morning, a Paludrine tablet was taken and every evening we would change out of shorts into long trousers and roll our shirtsleeves down at sunset. If a soldier contracted malaria then it was considered to be his own fault and after recovery, possibly put on report with a charge of self-inflicting wounds.

There was no need for mosquito nets in the highlands but something did bite me one night, on my lower eyelid. I didn't feel any pain and only noticed it when I looked in the mirror to shave. It just looked as though someone had pulled my eyelid open and placed a golf ball inside. It went down after an hour but it makes you think how many things there are in the tropics that want to eat you or get inside your body. Men, who came out of the ULU having been on patrol would tell us of things like the "bootlace snake"; its deadly and so small, it can get through the lace hole of a jungle boot. In addition, leeches that would gorge themselves on human blood had to be removed by touching them with a lit cigarette or pouring salt on them. Any other way, such as swiping them off your body, would cause infection, as the head of the leech would be left under the skin. There are also many types of spider, some that weave large webs across a trail and the unsuspecting would walk into the web and possibly receive a nasty bite. On the other hand, the giant centipede that crawls inside a sleeping bag can give a nasty bite. Scrub tics were potentially dangerous and had to be treated quickly otherwise paralysis could set in after a bite from one of those. What I did find about the creatures of the rainforest is, they will scurry off when they hear you coming and only bite when they feel threatened.

Charming People

We had a group of Malay soldiers/firemen attached to us, they were great guys and very likeable. I learned a lot of their way of life, including some of their language, culture and sport. When not on duty, I would play their game of badminton with them and became quite good but way out of their league. Another game was 'kipitup'. They stood in a circle and kicked a rattan ball (made from cane) up with the instep of their bare feet, passing it to each other while counting how many times they kept it up without touching the ground, hence 'kipitup'. They could do it for ages but when I joined in, it soon fell apart. However, they insisted that I always join them when a game was on. They were of the Muslim religion and only one or two practised it seriously throughout the year but when it came to Ramadam, they all took part. Ramadam is the holiest time in the Muslim calendar, their fasting period, which lasts a whole month; only water is taken during daylight hours. They had their own cook and obviously their own rations, which included meat that had been slaughtered in the traditional way according to their religion. Their meat had to be bled. I often had samples of their food, which I found quite delicious. They would use a lot of fruit in their curries and the curried fish was delightful.

Beautiful Creatures

One particular Malay, Hussein bin Rhamat would teach me jungle crafts and make me aware of what plants to avoid such as the Stinger Tree that could leave a nasty rash which lasted for months. We had many laughs on our walks when my jungle hat would be suddenly snatched from my head by the Lawyer Vine, commonly known as the Wait-a-while plant with its many hooks and spines down its long trailing fronds above head height. I would turn around and see my hat dangling in mid air. Hussein was only about 24 but his skill and knowledge of plants, wild life and jungle craft amazed me. We became good friends and he would take me for long walks, pointing out many different plants in the rainforest that were edible, medicinal or had other uses. In addition, several small animals such as the Malaysian black bear and orang-utans, which the Malays called 'Man of the Jungle'. There were also tree shrews and the large wild cat, which he called 'The Lance Corporal Cat' because it had a white chevron under its nose.

We would often swim in waterfalls but the water's temperature was quite cold, being so high up in the mountains. Hussein taught me how to catch and handle many of the numerous snakes and I became very adept at catching them with my bare hands, some of them like the krait, the pit viper and cobra were very poisonous. However, the python, although it could give a nasty bite, wasn't venomous, it killed its prey by squeezing the life out of them. They fed mostly on rats, which is why they were often seen near populated areas. However, I have seen a Python so big that it swallowed a large domestic pig then it went to sleep for a week, as it couldn't move. The locals tied it up to a long piece of bamboo and it took four men to carry it on their shoulders. I don't know what became of the python but the Chinese would like to get their hands on them to make folk law medicines.

The most interesting and beautiful creatures I thought, were the butterflies. There were millions of them and so many varieties, some as big as birds, like the swallowtail with its very long and colourful tails. They rested during the night close to a source of light and anyone who wanted to make a collection could just pick them off a wall or lamppost. Many years later, I was sad to see as many as twenty butterflies embedded in a plastic tray and sold as ornaments. They were bought in the thousands from cheap shops world-wide by stupid people who had no idea what they were doing. The business would have created a short-lived income for the poor people living in the jungle, by collecting them and selling them to dealers. Nevertheless, at the same time it decimated the wildlife population, such as the praying mantis, chameleons and other animals in the food chain who fed on the butterflies and moths. I went back to Malaya for a holiday with my wife thirty-five years later. We had a walk through the rainforests of the Cameron Highlands and did not see one butterfly during our half day's walk. Although the logging companies had not touched the jungle in the highlands, I noticed a marked difference in the absence of wildlife. Many of the giant two hundred feet tall hardwoods were still around, surrounded by thick undergrowth, but the once thriving forest seemed very quiet now and it left me feeling somewhat disappointed.

The Great Lover

Although the Malays were of a smaller stature than the average European, some of them enjoyed bodybuilding and keeping themselves in shape. Our boss had an old narrow gauge railway axle complete with iron wheels, brought up the mountain for us to train with. We used it as a weightlifter's barbell and would raise it in one clean jerk above our heads. My two years on the Dray wagons had left me in good shape and I was quite strong. I got the feeling that Hussein looked upon me as his role model; he would practise most days to eventually match the repetitions I could do. It was all good training for our job of manhandling equipment. The boss also got us to rig up a boxing ring inside the fire station where we had regular training bouts. The Malays didn't enjoy this kind of contact sport and it eventually fell by the wayside.

I walked into the ablutions one day and found Hussein doing something to his private parts with a small gold safety pin. After my initial shock, he explained, he would soon be going on leave in a few weeks and he was preparing himself by making a small hole in the loose skin below the front end of his penis. When the wound had healed, he would tie a piece of Horsehair through the hole in the shape of a bow. Apparently, when he goes home and makes love to one of the village girls, she would experience complete pleasure and tell all her friends how Hussein has become a great lover, thus giving him a wonderful fortnight leave. If all this were true, he would probably need another week to recover.

A face from the past

Lying on my bed one afternoon, I heard the daily convoy arriving and within minutes, my billet door opened and a suitcase, kitbag and webbing pack were thrown in. A body quickly followed with a face I knew from the past. I couldn't believe my eyes; it was Andy Ferguson, and a lad I had sat next to in school. He told me he had been posted to Station Lines as our new cook. We only ever had one cook at a time (with the help of a local from the village) in the little camp and we had all fed quite well in the past. However, over the next few months Andy excelled in his skills and I in particular received a bit of special attention as an old mate. The two of us were talking one day in the cookhouse when Andy asked me to reach up to the top shelf in the pantry and bring down a bag of flour. Being much taller, I reached up and pulled the sack forward, we could both see an enormous spider stretched out on the wall behind. I in particular had never seen such a big one; it could have been fifteen inches across, with great black hairy legs and a pair of fangs like hypodermic needles. 'It looks like a tarantula to me Andy' I said and gently tried to coax it into my hand. I had handled tarantula's before on my trips into the jungle with Hussein and knew they were not dangerous. They do bite if provoked or feel threatened but the bite is no worse than a bee sting. It seemed quite docile and I suddenly realised it wasn't alive, but still very fresh and flexible. 'Bloody hell Andy, this is a big one' I said turning around, with it stretched out between both hands. 'Andy, Andy' I called but couldn't see him anywhere. Eventually, I found him halfway across the parade ground, standing there in his whites and chef's hat, with a large frying pan in one hand and looking very pale with eyes as big as saucers. He eventually told me, before I arrived at the cookhouse, he had tried to get the sack of flour down off the high shelf himself with a brush handle, he must have pushed the sack forward and trapped the insect between the bag and the wall. The poor guy was in a state of panic and I realised he was suffering from arachnophobia, a fear of spiders. It took some time to entice him back into the cookhouse and over the next few weeks, Hussein and myself managed to coax Andy out of his fear by making him realise there was no real danger in most insects. In fact, he started having a big interest in all kinds of creatures that we brought out of the forest, as long as he saw us handling them, then he was happy to do the same. Someone came across two small black bears that had been abandoned in the forest; probably their mother had suffered at the hands of hunters. They were quite thin and obviously very hungry and they responded well to the care they were given. A week later, the bears were full of life, especially around five in the morning when they were chasing each other up and down the billet, bouncing from one bed to another with socks and boots in their mouths. The guys who looked after them managed to keep their secret for only a couple of weeks before the sergeant major found out and ordered them to be returned to the jungle. Sometimes it was like living inside a giant Zoo with all the creatures we kept coming across. I loved every minute of my life there.

Naked Maidens

Several tribes of Sakis, Malaya's indigenous people lived in the highlands. They were much smaller than the average Malay and lived in bamboo and attap houses raised on stilts. The Saki males were proficient hunters who used long blowpipes to send a poisonous dart high into the canopy to knock out their prey. I have watched as the diminutive, almost pygmy size man in front of me prepared his weapon by placing a dart in the tube then putting a small wad of natural cotton wool behind the dart. Lifting the very long bamboo pipe up towards the treetops and expanding his lungs to bursting point, before sending the dart with a blast of air to its target. The missile was too quick for my eye, what I did see, was the body of a large bird falling down through the branches and leaves towards us. The British Army often employed these hunters as trackers on their patrols in the jungle in search of the enemy, so clever were they at picking out the tiny clues left by a terrorist, no matter how slow and careful they had moved through the rain forest, even days before. Halfway down the road to Tapah, was a tribe where the women would bath every morning under the natural shower of a waterfall at the side of the road. When they heard the military convoy approaching, the women would cover their naked bodies momentarily until the trucks passed by. Their embarrassment was as a result of the catcalls and whistles from the troops in previous convoys. Nevertheless, to catch sight of the young nubile figures, the drivers would switch off their engines a few bends before they reached the waterfall. This free wheeling was all very well until one day there was a four truck pile up just beyond the bathing site, the drivers were all busy ogling which resulted in a few broken headlamps, tail lamps, bent bumpers and lots of skidmarks. They had a lot of explaining to do when they got back to camp and the usual part one orders materialised warning all drivers to keep their eyes on the road at all times

Guarding the Tea Plantation

with a mild threat of being put on OCs orders in any future occurrence. Nobody took any notice, the thrill of seeing young naked women bathing in the waterfall was too much. Only five days later, the same thing happened again but because there was a shortage of drivers and there was an emergency on, no action was started against the offenders.

Enter Elvis

One day I came across a praying mantis in the billet. These are wonderful insects that can be handled very easily. We decided to call it Elvis. I would have it sitting on one hand and pass it a live moth which it would grab with both front forearms and have a good feed. Afterwards Elvis would take meticulous care in cleaning every bit of its forearms, with its very dextrous

111

mouth and tongue. Then I would offer it a drink of water from a teaspoon, which it took gladly. The Mantis lived quite happily in the billet, usually on a high windowsill where it kept itself quite still until the next feeding time. We had a few tame cats that lived in and around the camp. They would pick up titbits from guys coming out of the cookhouse. The cats had a habit of wandering into various billets looking for a stroke or tickle under the chin. It was on one such occasion that Elvis nearly died. A cat had wandered into the billet and spotted the insect. The feline hunter bounded up, using one of the beds as a springboard and lunged onto the windowsill, which was five or six feet off the ground. It grabbed Elvis in its mouth and was down on the floor in all of about one and a half seconds. I grabbed the cat in less time by the scruff of the neck with one hand and forced its jaws open with the other. One of the cat's fangs had pierced a wing cover and was stopping the insect from dropping out. While I kept hold of the cat, Bill gently took hold of Elvis and freed him from the cat's mouth. As soon as I let go of the cat, it shot out of the hut quicker than you could blink; it really didn't enjoy being held by the scruff of the neck. Elvis soon recovered and carried on with his normal routine for a few months until he went missing. We immediately thought the bloody cat has had him and we resigned ourselves to life without our favourite pet. Several weeks later, we had to give the billet a spring clean in preparation for a flying visit by the Regimental Sergeant Major (RSM) who only made one visit a year. I was standing on a chair cleaning the windowpanes when I saw another Preying Mantis tucked into a corner. It was well camouflaged against the light green paintwork and seemed to be wriggling, on closer inspection, I could see about a dozen tiny Mantises close by with some crawling over its body. They were perfect miniatures of the big one; furthermore, there was a hole in one of the parents wing covers. It was our Elvis and he'd had babies. I couldn't contain myself and dashed into the fire station shouting 'Elvis is back, and he's a mother!' All the lads in hearing distance came over to have a look, everyone had known Elvis and they were all in buoyant mood after that day. Someone said, 'You will have to give it a new name now that you know it's female'. 'Bugger off,' we all said, 'If Elvis wanted to change his sex then it was up to him'.

Night Attack

Towards the middle of July in our first year, the Monsoons came one afternoon as I was playing badminton with the Malays. I heard a noise from the treetops like an express train coming. We stopped playing and focussed on the jungle canopy that surrounded the camp. I couldn't believe my eyes and ears and was momentarily transfixed by the amount of water that was falling out of the sky. It was almost like a waterfall that was spilling itself over some invisible plateaux and coming across the camp at speed. We made a dash for the billets, which were about a hundred yards away. I made it to the door just in time. Ginger was already inside, lying on his bed reading, he looked at me in shock and shouted at the top of his voice, "What the hell is that?" as rain and hail battered on the tin roof in a thunderous roar. This was our first experience of a monsoon storm and we were to see many more before the dry season returned. It did get quite exciting some days when great cracks of fork lightening came down and bounced off the carpark, followed by enormously loud rolls of thunder. Most soldiers owned an umbrella that was made from bamboo and varnished paper. They cost cents to buy but were an invaluable piece of equipment to have when walking to and from the cookhouse or NAAFI. One afternoon, all four occupants of our little billet were lying on top of our beds, reading. A storm was playing itself out overhead, we were trying to decide whose turn it was to fetch tiffin from the cookhouse. Tiffin was afternoon tea and sandwiches, which we had at about three o'clock. We took it in turns to take our four mugs, make four sandwiches from the bread, margarine and tinned sardines or pilchards that were always laid out. They liked my sandwiches because I would put plenty of pepper and a sprinkle of vinegar on them.

Before we could decide whose turn it was there was an almighty bang and one of the lads was lifted off his bed and landed on the floor three feet away. He was still holding his book in both hands. A bolt of lightening had hit the electrical fuse box on the wall above his head and the explosion had caused a shockwave big enough to lift him bodily through the air. He wasn't hurt but we ended up with a big hole in the gable end of the billet and no electricity. We were all fortunate to have good quality latex mattresses and this is probably what saved his life as the lightening could have gone through his body and iron bed on its journey to earth.

Some weeks later, during a quiet period in atmospheric activity, we were awakened in the middle of the night and realised it had been a gunshot. It was so loud and seemed to have been right outside the door. A Lee Enfield .303 rifle makes a big bang when it's discharged. I still suffer with Tinnitus, a constant ringing in the ears caused by my early days on the firing range. Ear defenders had not been issued to us and after a days shooting practice we all suffered. "F***inell, we're being attacked" I shouted as we all grabbed our rifles. Within seconds, the whole camp was on the alert and we discovered the cause of the gunshot. Louie Lomax was on perimeter guard duty and had seen a terrorist through the wire, twenty yards away in the undergrowth, and he was signalling with his raised hand to his comrades to attack the camp. Louie took aim and shot him. The remainder of the guard and several others with weapons did a search of the area outside the fence but not a trace was found of any terrorists. It was realised, what he had seen was a leaf, gently moving in the breeze. Louie got a new nickname after that incident and was known as Leafy Lomax.

Terrorists in the Tea Plantation

Some armed terrorists entered the Boh Tea Plantation one morning; they were looking for food. The plantation manager made a hurried and urgent call to the police station in Tanah Rata but the station was undermanned that day. Federation Police in the Highlands were fully armed and trained by the British in jungle warfare, but most of them were already out on some sort of mission. The emergency had been passed onto the nearest unit to the plantation, which happened to be us. Our small camp consisted of rear echelons; i.e. we were not a front line force. The next thing that happened, Sergeant Stevens gathered as many odds and sods together. The motley crew comprised of six MT drivers, two mechanics and myself, a fireman. We bundled ourselves into two Landrovers and headed down the mountain road. Sergeant Stevens, whose normal job was being in charge of the motor transport, was preparing himself mentally for the attack. Finally, he thought he'd better make sure our weapons were ready for the job, he fired his Sten Gun, a short burst through the open doorway, (some vehicles didn't have doors on them) then shouted back to us to fire two shots each into the Jungle. It's a good job no other traffic was on the road; there could have been mayhem as we all started firing at once. Five minutes later we arrived at the plantation. The Manager was waiting for us and said, "That was a good idea, the terrorists all fled when they heard your guns firing". Sergeant Stevens, who was a bit of a Gung Ho character looked quite disappointed at losing his chance of a bravery medal. He instructed us to carry out a search of the premises and surrounding area. I went inside with a few others to search from top to bottom of the three-story building. The place was clear of anyone other than Indian workers who were getting on with their jobs. I was very interested by the process of tea production. The fresh green leaves were brought in from the fields, placed on large canvas frames and left for many days to dry naturally until they turned brown and crispy, after which, they were lightly crushed and graded. The whole place was very antiquated, a man who dropped shovels full of dried leaves into the slipstream of an electric fan carried out the grading. Heavier particles dropped quickly while lighter ones were carried further down the room.

Inside the Tea Factory

The result being, a long pile of perfectly graded tea from best quality to fine dust. His assistant used a broom to keep the pile together. I noticed how both men, dressed in no more than loincloths, were constantly chewing betel nuts and leaves, which are a mild euphoric stimulant. I hadn't noticed the red stains on the wooden floor until one of them spat out a great globule of spittle. It was everywhere, on the stairs and on each floor including the packing room floor. The product of the betel tree increases a person's work capacity when chewed. I suppose this is the reason why the manager allowed it to go on. All the employees were of Indian origin and betel nuts are a part of their culture and religion. The manager was so grateful with our quick response that he made a presentation to each of us, of two, one-pound packets of his best tea while putting his hands together and bowing to each of us in turn. I sent mine home to mother and never mentioned the betel nut incident. I was very reluctant to drink tea for many years after that day, then as I grew older I thought, 'What the hell, tea always gets made with boiling water so it must be safe'.

Forest Fire

After that incident, Sgt Stevens persuaded the CO that we needed a firing range to give the troops some shooting practice. Because we always had plenty of time on our hands, the fire service was given the job of felling enough trees in a small valley on the south perimeter of the camp. No mechanical saws were available and it all had to be done using a hand operated chain saw, which was something like a bicycle chain with teeth and a handle each end. In addition, of course, we had plenty of axes. It was hard work and it took us several weeks between helicopter standbys and the occasional call out, to fell an area of about forty to fifty square metres. It was an awesome sight to see the giant two hundred foot trees crashing to the ground, quite often bringing smaller and weaker ones with them as a result of the web of thick vines high up in the canopy. I also felt a bit sad to see these living plants that could have been over two hundred years of age coming to the end of their lives and with them, the habitats of a multitude of small creatures of the rain forest. Just as we were wondering how to dispose of the felled trees, our boss received a signal from the CO of some fighting unit asking if we could safely dispose of forty four gallons of flame throwing fuel for which they had no further use. Our boss was delighted with the request, 'We can burn the felled trees' he said. Within a few days, we took delivery of the fuel, which was in four-gallon cans. Flame throwing fuel is a highly combustible jelly like substance. With me having long legs, it fell to yours truly to climb over the fallen trees, starting at the far end, and pour the stuff over as many trunks as possible. 'Use it all Kelly, we don't want any left over' he shouted as I struggled. The remainder of the crew, all Malayan, were standing guard making sure no source of ignition came within a hundred yards of the fuel. As I worked backwards pouring can after can over the area, I was in a lather of sweat. I think most of it was from my own fearful thoughts that I could go up with this lot any minute. I poured the final can of fuel as a long trail out towards the road where everyone from the camp had come to watch. Sgt Russ, my boss asked the CO if he would like the honour of setting it alight. 'No thank you Sgt Russ, I think that honour should go to fireman Kelly, he was the one mad enough to go out there' 'Thanks Sir' I replied as I bent down, struck the match and joined the rest behind cover. The flame raced along the ground until it reached the area where a massive invisible cloud of explosive vapour hung over the fallen trees. It went up like a mini atom bomb, lifting trees weighing many tons momentarily off the ground while smaller debris shot up through a mushroom of cloud and flame, high into the afternoon sky. "F***kinell" We all said together as we felt the heat from the now raging fire which started to spread up a small hill to our right. It was heading for the oil storage shed and we were forced to bring the pumps into action to dampen things down. The fire burned all night and did exactly what was wanted. Within a few more weeks, the firing range was set up and I among all the others enjoyed shooting a variety of weapons, the Bren Machine Gun being my favourite. Sgt Stevens was in his element; he had taken charge of the shooting range and had set up a variety of targets including beer cans, old shoes and a teddy bear that were all hanging from a line. Apart from a couple of rounds near the tea plantation, the last time I had fired a weapon was off the stern end of the troopship halfway across the Indian Ocean. They had thrown over some coloured balloons with a bit of water in them to weigh them down and we had to wait until they were about a hundred yards away before firing. It was very difficult with them bouncing up and down on the ship wake, I didn't hit a single one and finished up with a ringing in the ears again. I was prepared for the noise this time by stuffing some four by two in my ears. Four by two is a dimension of flannelette that is used to clean the inside of the barrel of our weapons.

To catch a Monkey

I was sent to Singapore on a course for two weeks, to brush up on skills in firefighting; this was a preliminary to promotion. The camp at Singapore was near the sea and I went canoeing one day along the many tributaries at the back of the camp. I have a good sense of direction and was confident that I could find my way back but I did not take into account the tide going out. The rivers and tributaries that had plenty of water when I set off, were now down to mere trickles with great mud banks each side. I had extreme difficulty paddling and when finally getting near my original start point, had to wade, waste deep through mud, dragging the canoe behind me to the top of the bank. The sun was so hot that by the time I put the canoe away and walked back to my billet, the thick mud had baked hard around my legs like a couple of drain pipes. A troop of wild apes lived in a large tree near our barrack block in Singapore. One of the camps permanent staff showed me how to catch one; we borrowed a pair of large strong leather gauntlets from a motorcycle despatch rider. A few peanuts were placed in a bottle and a long cord tied around the neck of the bottle, this was placed on the ground under the tree. Very soon, the troop of apes would come down to investigate, one of the young ones would eventually put its hand inside and grab some nuts. The cord was then pulled and all the monkeys except the one holding the peanuts would scream and run back up the tree. The one with its hand in the bottle wouldn't have the sense to open its hand and drop the nuts and would soon be caught by the guy wearing the gauntlets. Lots of drivers kept small monkeys as pets and would have them fastened with a thin chain around their waist. The animals would be well looked after; they soon became tame and made good pets. They also had the freedom of the truck cab, determined by the length of the chain. They seemed to like riding outside on the top more than anywhere else or out on one of the rear view mirrors.

When I got back to the Cameron Highlands, a new man was in charge. Warrant Officer Smalley had replaced Sergeant Bert Russ who had returned to the UK.

This new man seemed to have very little skill in man management and very quickly got the backs up of everyone, especially the normally placid and easy going Malay soldiers. Our lives changed dramatically for the worse and pretty soon, some of the Malays applied for a transfer. They had never experienced the sort of mindless discipline that he metred out. He was obviously on some sort of power kick and wanted to show us all that he was the boss. One morning, I saw one of the Malay soldiers splitting open a plant-like pod of some description, and he was sprinkling the almost invisible contents on the boss's desk. He told me it was a type of itching powder that grew in the Jungle and would get into his skin and forearms giving him a really bad time; I had other things to attend to and left him to do what he had to. I enjoyed Army life and just got on with it, no matter what I was asked to do and I did it with enthusiasm. I was determined that nobody was going to ruin my pleasure of being out here in the Far East.

Match Postponed

We were given the job of removing a large hornets nest from the attic of a nearby house, where the Commanding Officer and his wife lived. I had to don breathing apparatus and enter the walk in attic with some smoke bombs. In the dark, I could hear the hornets buzzing all around me. My body had been well and truly covered up from head to toe with two boiler suits, two balaclavas and strong gloves and goggles. Treading very gently across the floor joists I approached the enormous hive hanging down from a roof beam. The torch on my breathing apparatus showed it to be about two-foot across and three feet deep. It must have housed millions of the creatures. I had three smoke bombs on a steel tray, which I placed directly beneath the hive and set them going. The smoke devices burn intensely when they're working, giving off great volumes of acrid smoke and they make a fizzing and spluttering sound. The hornets were quick to respond as the noise from them intensified. I made my way for the exit and slammed the door behind me but not before missing one of the joists and putting my foot through the ceiling below. It happened to be a spare bedroom that wasn't used. Outside, about five hundred metres away, two football teams were playing a match on the Padang. The Hornets swarmed out of the roof of the house like a big dark cloud and flew en-mass for the moving objects on the pitch to avenge their anger. A river ran alongside the football ground and within minutes both complete teams, the linesmen, referee, and several spectators were in the water up to their necks. I went back into the attic again to recover the steel plate and what was left of the smoke bombs; literally thousands of the insects had sacrificed their lives by attacking the flames. The steel tray was full of them. The rest of the crew were standing by to dispose of the hive but they never got chance as the swarm came back again. We were told to abandon the task and return to camp. We heard later that the CO and his family had to move elsewhere that night.

Virginity lost

There was a small Catholic Church in the area and sometimes I would go to Mass on a Sunday morning. A beautiful young Chinese girl with rosebud mouth and almond eyes caught my attention every time I went there. Lots of Chinese people became Christians and those women who normally have to wear a hat in church would have instead, a little embroidered headpiece pinned to their hair. This made them look very feminine and graceful; especially the girl who was now making advanced eyes at me every week.

I was still quite shy and had no worldly experience of wooing but I could feel my hormones reaching new levels. Eventually, she made the first approach one Sunday as we were leaving and introduced herself as Lin Yao. She could speak quite good English and wanted to know more about me and where I came from. The following week, the same thing happened, I walked her home to her father's fruit and vegetable farm. Lin told me there would be nobody home on Sundays as her mother would be visiting relatives and her father would be playing Majong with his friends in the village. It was a gorgeous sunny afternoon as we walked around the fields of fresh vegetables of every description. We came to a large area of luscious strawberries and she invited me to taste them, they were so sweet and delicious. I couldn't remember having tasted fresh strawberries before then; they had always come out of a jam jar. We sat down and talked for a long time. Lin Yao was very inquisitive and asked questions about my past and where I lived and about my first job. I told her about the pawnbroker's, she couldn't understand the concept of pawnbroking and wanted to learn more. I was doing my best to explain and was telling her about the symbol of a pawnbroker being Three Brass Balls; she edged closer and looked quizzically into my eyes. "I don't understand, what is brass?" she said, I got the scent of a beautiful perfume she was wearing which caught me off balance. Our faces were getting closer and closer. "Golden, Golden balls," I whispered, our faces were an inch away and I could feel myself tingling with a new sensation. "Do you mean these?" she whispered in a low voice and placed her gentle hand at the top of my leg. I could never have imagined the feeling of ecstasy that suddenly overtook me; within minutes we were embracing passionately and making love. Up to that moment, I had been the original 'Virgin Soldier', I was nearly twenty years old and this was my first time. Afterwards, we were laying back, she was picking more of the soft fruit and popping them into my mouth, I thought I was in heaven and at the same time feeling very mature at having suddenly reached manhood. I was also trying to fight back the memory of words I'd heard earlier from someone saying, "The most important wish in a Chinese girls mind is getting married to a British soldier, this is their ticket to freedom and the western world". When we parted, little did I know, it would be the last time I saw Lin Yao. The hand of fate took control, events overtook me and soon after, I left the Cameron Highlands forever.

Only a week before, I had lost my buddy Ginger, no, a Commie hadn't slotted him, his National Service time was up and he was going home for demobilisation. The last I saw of him was in the back of a Bedford Truck, one of those in a convoy heading out of camp. He was a really nice guy from Nottingham. He was also an only child and his mother doted on him. She would regularly send him parcels and he would also receive six editions of the Daily Mirror Newspaper every week. By the time they arrived, they would be well out of date but we all read them with enthusiasm. I was nearly bowled over one day when I came across a large picture in the paper of my childhood sweetheart, Elaine O'Brien in a swimsuit. We had been next-door neighbours and played together as toddlers. At the age of nine, her parents took her to live in the Isle of Man. Elaine grew up to be a Croupier in Britain's first gambling Casino in Douglas I.o.M. She had blossomed into a beautiful young woman with a figure to match. She was pictured in a bathing costume on a beach and it was obvious, the newspaper photographer had coaxed her into a striking pose. The reason she was in the news was industrial action by the Casino's employees. All my mates were jealous but they had no reason to be, she had gone out of my life a long time ago but I did keep her pin-up picture on my locker for a while.

Ginger and I had come a long way together, we had been good buddies and all of a sudden, I felt lonely for the first time in my life. The only other British soldier in my unit was the boss, a Warrant Officer. Soldiers and senior ranks did not mix or converse in those days other than to give or take orders. It suddenly dawned on me that I had another year to spend up here in the mountains and I was not particularly looking forward to it.

A Sad loss

After Ginger had gone home, I must have been letting things get on top of me. We had just lost a friend, one of the Kings Dragoon Guards in a shooting accident. He was waiting in his armoured car at the front of the convoy that was about to leave. He had loaded his two Bren Guns which were mounted on the top of his vehicle and forgetting that he'd cocked them, did some last minute adjustment to the inboard trigger mechanism while sitting outside the vehicle, on top of his Cupola. He overtightened the adjustment screw to the trigger, one of the machine guns started firing on automatic. The gun spun round as the bullets were ricocheting off the ground in the car park. Everybody dived for cover but the last four rounds from the magazine of twenty-eight ripped into his waist. It all happened so quickly. The wound was enormous and he bled to death within a very short time. Instead of escorting the convoy down the mountain, his body made its last journey in the back of one of the trucks a day or so later. It affected us all because he was a young good looking guy who was well liked.

Crime and punishment 2

As a result of allowing the drink to take hold of me on the Saturday night, I ended up in the Guardhouse. The following morning, I was marched in front of the Commanding Officer to answer to the charge of striking a non-commissioned officer. It was a load of nonsense, I never struck anybody but I did push him and he fell against a wall and went down on his backside. It was completely out of character for me, I had no excuse and took my punishment of ten days detention. There was no facility to hold detainees for more than a day in the tiny mountain top camp and I was taken down to a camp in the lowlands seventy-five miles away at Ipoh. Waking up behind bars is definitely not recommended. Oh my word, what have I done? A few days ago, I was halfway through a junior NCOs cadre, my boss had great hopes for me and had recommended me for promotion. I had just found a new girlfriend and lover then as a result of going out with a few lads from the Transport Company, they weren't really good mates either, and having too much to drink, I tried to defend one of them from a Military Police Sergeant. The MP was giving the lad a dressing down for something or nothing and by his manner was showing all the mindless dogmatic control that these types of people thrived on. The lad answered back, the Sergeant drew his baton. Through my drunken eyes, I could see once more, a picture of my old school teacher wielding his big stick, and my mind just snapped and I finished up getting arrested.

The next ten days started very badly, I wasn't used to the heat and extreme humidity of the lowlands. When people arrived in Malaya, they were usually given a week for their systems to acclimatise to the temperatures before starting any duties. For me, coming down off the mountaintop it was hell on earth. There were three other guys in the cells, one of them was from Cheltenham and he was a rebel who had previously set fire to his mattress in the cell. The Provo Police had given him a hard time and he was now buckling down and behaving himself. We were made to run everywhere, the sweat poured out of

3 tonner

me, but I wouldn't let them see it was hurting. In fact, after a few days, I actually started enjoying it. The rebel on remand was waiting for trial accused of murder, having allegedly hit a rickshaw driver over the head with a rock. A few days after I arrived, he disappeared, his cell was empty and we heard on the camp grapevine that he had been posted to Germany. Obviously the trial never took place, the life of some poor little rickshaw driver wasn't as important as the reputation of her Majesty's Armed Forces. I must have lost nearly a stone in weight. By the time I got out, I was lean, fit, strong and very irascible.

New life of adventure

With my Army career in tatters, I was transferred from the fire service and posted to 27 Company RASC. This was a transport unit in Kuala Lumpur where it was said, they posted all the lads that had been in trouble, a sort of penal battalion, and now I was one of them.

I hadn't been there an hour before I challenged a big mouth Jock who was giving some little guy a hard time just outside my Basha (hut made of leaves and bamboo). Without thinking, it seemed such a natural thing to do. The bully was mouthing obscenities into the face of someone I didn't even know. It was the continuous noise that was annoying me. Finally, I got up off my bed, went outside and said "Hey big mouth, sling your f*** king hook", an old Liverpool Dockers term meaning 'Go away'. The bully backed off. I think it was the combination of my height, my accent and the grim look on my face. At that moment in time it would probably have scared anyone off. I didn't have a friend in this strange new place until I walked into the NAAFI later that night. Someone was beckoning me over to a table full of blokes, they all had smiles and looks of approval on their faces. One of them passed me a bottle of beer and said "Thanks Scouse, we've been waiting for someone to sort him out". Without knowing, I had challenged the top dog who had been bullying the camp for a long time and most importantly for me, he had backed down. From that moment on, my life was great, I had many new friends who showed me a lot of respect and nobody got bullied in that camp as long as I was there. My reputation was all that was needed; after all, not many men have floored a Military Police Sergeant.

I enjoyed my new life as a transport driver, which took me all over Malaya. On many occasions, I went on attachment to various other regiments for several weeks at a time. I've been with the SAS who were a mad lot but good company. We would parade in the morning and I was surprised to see such a motley group of men wearing different caps and badges. This Special Air Service unit was in its infancy. They were all trained parachutists from various regiments and had volunteered to belong to a very elite fighting force. My lorry would be loaded with ration packs, fresh water, ammunition and clean uniforms. With a couple of armed men in the back and one in the front, we would set off on some mysterious route through miles of narrow jungle tracks and eventually stop at some feature like a crossroads or river bend. I'd switch off the engine and we'd take all round defensive positions and wait. Shortly, some figures would appear out of the forest, they looked emaciated and filthy; this was a patrol of the Special Air Service who had rendezvoused with us for supplies. I don't know how long they had been in the jungle but by their appearance, it must have been several weeks or even months. Back at camp there was always lots of activity from men preparing kit, cleaning and test firing weapons, and groups huddled together over maps. On other occasions, I would be with the Gurkha Regiment; they are wonderful little men from Nepal in the Himalayan foothills of Mount Everest. They were always very smart and extremely proud to be serving with the British Army. If a Gurkha soldier was ever reprimanded for some minor indiscretion then his punishment was to be taken off his next guard duty. They considered it a great honour to be on guard duty, especially on the main gate where they would be seen bristling with pride. The Kukri knife the Gurkha wore would be razor sharp and tradition says that it must never be taken out of its sheath without drawing blood. You would often see a small plaster on one of the fingers of those who kept the tradition going. They were excellent jungle fighters and feared by the Communist Terrorists. The Gurkhas were used during the Japanese occupation and many of the Japs had been decapitated with one quick slice of the Kukri blade, particularly the last man in a Jap patrol walking along a jungle path at twilight. Imagine the shock felt by the rest of the Japanese soldiers when they made their gruesome discovery. The Gurkha assassin would have been well gone by then. I would take my truck with two of the Gurkhas on board, to pick up fresh rations from some supply depot. Once a week we picked up live goats, sheep, and sometimes young bullocks. Back at the camp, I'd watch them being slaughtered. They'd hoist up a sheep or goat by their back legs. A large aluminium tray was placed underneath. After saying a small prayer, the slaughter man would take the animal's head off with one quick swipe of his extremely sharp machete, leaving the meat to be perfectly bled. The bullocks being too big to hoist up were left to stand with their heads tethered to a post, while the same procedure was carried out but with a much bigger and heavier knife. It was an amazing spectacle to see the knife severing the head from the body in one clean action. The slaughterer was an extremely powerful man who treated all the animals in a very humanely and kind manner up to the point of death. A log of timber was placed on the ground between the animal's front legs to stop the blade being blunted as it hit the ground. My two companions became quite excited one day; it was the monthly rum ration. I watched as the Gurkha Quartermaster in a large white apron opened a cask of rum and poured the contents into a larger empty half barrel. He filled the cask up with tap water, swirled it around a couple of times and poured that into the open barrel. Then taking a big wooden paddle; he stirred the mix up for several minutes. A queue of Gurkha soldiers had formed each with an empty bottle and two Ringits (Malay dollars) in their hands. My friends had bought a bottle for me as well. The rum in the cask was one hundred percent proof and had to be watered down otherwise it would have blown their heads off. The three of us sat drinking and chatting for an hour and I was surprised how easily it was going down. By the time we left, I was also surprised to see we had got through two bottles of rum between the three of us. I still had to park the truck up and suddenly my legs didn't feel like they were mine. It took me some effort to climb up into the cab. Somehow, I drove the truck the two hundred yards to the motor Transport Park. To me, it seemed as though the steering had gone as I bounced off banking to my right. I'd never been drunk behind the wheel before and would certainly not recommend it. After switching the engine off, I fell out onto the ground and lay there until one of the night guards woke me at midnight. Those Gurkha boys must have been used to rum but I had never been a big drinker and the following morning had one almighty headache and hangover and had missed my breakfast. It put me off drinking rum and getting drunk for the rest of my life. Getting drunk means you are not in control of yourself and I didn't like that. The first time I got drunk, I landed up in jail. I decided there and then that I was not going to make a habit of it. Another assignment I had been given was picking up ex-prisoners from a big military prison on the morning of their release. Men from all three services would be in jail serving a variety of awards (that's what Commanding Officers say when they hand out a sentence, "I award you twenty eight days" or whatever the sentence was). I would then take freed prisoner to the Railway Station or back to their own camp if it wasn't too far away.

They'd tell me about life inside the prison where men would shave the hairs off their legs and mix it with what little tobacco they had to make their roll-ups go further. As they were not allowed matches, they devised a way of getting a light from the electric bulb holder. They would cut the bottom off a toothpaste tube (they were made of aluminium in those days) open it up like a little canoe, place in some fluff from a blanket and pour in a little metal polish. It was then placed in a groove that had been cut in the top of the broom handle and gently lifted up to make contact with the two prongs of a light socket. A quick flash of electric current would set the fluff burning. Most of the time, a fuse somewhere in the prison would blow and they had to get their fags smoked quickly before the guards came to investigate. Some guys have been so desperate they'd drunk a can of metal polish for its alcohol content. One morning, I picked up a Royal Navy sailor who had more tattoos than anyone I had ever seen. I was taking him to Kuala Lumpur Railway Station but he never got there. He jumped out of the lorry at a stop sign and ran like the wind towards Batu Road, the notorious red light district. As far as anyone else was concerned, I had dropped him off at the Station. There was a big river near the camp where we sometimes washed our trucks on Friday afternoons by driving them into the shallow waters. The elephant keepers would also be there, washing their big working animals after a day's logging in the forest. I tried my Malay language on one of the keepers and he got his elephant to swill off my truck by using its trunk. It was a wonderful sight, to see the big animal sucking up water and spaying it over the four-ton truck as though it just knew what to do. I never did possess a camera in those days and if I had, I'm sure I would have had many wonderful photographs, all in black and white of course, colour film had not been invented.

End of the Troubles

Malaya got its independence and the troubles ceased on 31st August 1957. We all received a medal with our number rank and name imprinted on the edge. I knew two guys who immediately sold theirs to a dealer in the town for the equivalent of a couple of pounds each. Apparently, the medals have a high silver content. The end of the conflict also meant we could go out in civilian clothes for the very first time since coming to Malaya. I enjoyed going into the city of Kuala Lumpur on Saturday nights to an air-conditioned cinema. I wasn't able to understand the Chinese film being shown but it was heaven sitting in a cool environment for an hour or so. Then I would go exploring the many Chinese and Indian shops that were festooned with goods. In fact, there was not a spare square foot in these places. We could spend an hour looking around the millions of items for something special that we wanted to take back to the UK. I paid for a beautiful delicate Bone China Tea Service. Every piece was hand painted, showing a black rose. The shopkeeper parcelled it up for me and sent it home to my mother, she had it until she died at the age of ninety-two, then it came back into my possession. Lots of traders operated on the edge of pavements with the most basic of equipment. We could get measured up for a pair of shoes or a shirt, they would be ready in a couple of hours, and they would be a perfect fit. Every shop had one little space reserved for a Temple, where burning Josh sticks and candles were gently smouldering in front of religious figures. When they finally closed for the night, the staff would sleep on bamboo and rope beds on the pavement outside. After a few drinks, we would go back to camp by rickshaw and have a meal of some description at one of the eating stalls outside the back of the camp. My favourite dish was Nasi Goring, a dish of fried rice, egg and prawns. In the early hours of Sunday morning, there could be twenty or more soldiers sitting, eating, drinking and quietly talking in these eating stalls run by the locals. The lads had been out, had a good time and spent their energy in the city and I always considered it quality time to have lighthearted discussion about any and everything in life under the constant hiss of the kerosene lamps overhead.

A Dangerous Swim

Our unit went on a re-training exercise to the east coast wilderness area of Malaya. The journey was very interesting as I was on the advance party and we had to get there and build a tented camp for the rest of the company who were to follow in a week's time. One big river we came to (the Kuantan) had to be crossed using pontoons. This meant driving two trucks at a time onto a floating pontoon, which was then powered across by a Sampan (small boat) with an outboard motor. It took hours to ferry the dozen trucks across and some guys decided to cool down by having a swim in the river. The locals were shouting something from across the other side; I could just make out the Malay word BUAYA, which they kept shouting, BUAYA, BUAYA. I was racking my brain, I knew the word but couldn't remember what it meant. Then it came to me, CROCODILE! I shouted to the lads in the water, all of a sudden, they were as good as Olympic champions. "Fucking hell Scouse, where?" one of them said, as he got out of the water, his eyes were as big as pan lids. I spent three glorious weeks at our wilderness camp on the South China Sea. We swam in the crystal clear ocean every day and climbed Coconut trees to get at the fruit; well it was me who climbed. They knew I had been a Fireman, and had thrown down the challenge. Five minutes later and thirty feet up, I was holding on with one arm wrapped securely around the tree and screwing the big nuts around several times to break the strong stalk that was holding them on. Four mates were down below holding each corner of a blanket.

133

The first two nuts had split open when we allowed them to fall on the sand and it was the juice we were after. I felt a twinge on my left arm and looked to see what it was. I got the shock of my life, a whole army of big ferocious looking red ants where marching along my arm, heading for my neck and they were starting to bite. I shinned down so fast; I skinned my chest, inside thighs and arms on the rough bark of the tree and dashed across the red-hot burning sands to dive into the sea. The South China Sea was the most beautiful I have ever come across. Myriads of fish swam in the crystal blue water and we spent all our free time swimming or just lazing about in the gentle surf. Apart from the training aspect, it was like paradise on earth. One day, we had to camouflage our trucks along the edges of a big clearing. Drivers were chopping down saplings to conceal their vehicles but I had a better idea, I reversed mine into the bush, there's not much to damage the rear end of a four tonner. When it was far enough in, the trees and bushes at the sides sprang back into position and there was very little else to do but put a few branches at the front and it was perfectly cammed up.

One of my mates, little Lennie Barnard from Devon thought he'd do the same, but he didn't go into the bush first to check the ground and finished up sinking his truck into a hidden bog. It was tilted back about forty-five degrees and looked strange with is windscreens pointing skywards. It took four other lorries with chains, pulling together and the rest of the day before we got his truck out.

The isolation got to one of the boys one night and he decided to take a truck to town, the nearest village was forty-five miles away. I was asked to drive the Landrover with our Lieutenant and another guy to find and bring him back. As we were leaving, a roll call was being taken to determine who the missing driver was. At ten thirty and after a long journey we arrived at Kampong Baharu. We soon spotted the truck parked outside a small bar. The three of us peered in through the window and the young lieutenant almost winced when he saw who it was, Gerry McGrath, he had done fifty six days in Changi Prison for stabbing a policeman in a pub brawl. He was sitting at a table with one hand around a bottle of beer and the other around a young Chinese slip of a girl who was sitting on his knee. "You know him Kelly," said the officer. "Go and get him to come outside, I don't want to provoke him in there". I went in and walked straight up to the bar not looking at McGrath, he saw me and shouted across "Scouse mate, what ye havin te drink" in a broad Glaswegen accent. He paid for my beer and I sat down beside him but opposite the window where I could see the officer and other soldier looking in through the glass. I took my time, enjoyed two beers with the compliments of Jock, and was eventually able to talk him into returning to camp. Once outside, the only way McGrath would come quiet was if I drove his truck back and he came with me as passenger. It was now nearly midnight and the Lieutenant told me to get my foot down. There were no road lights and no other traffic, after about five miles we came to the single-track wooden bridge. I swung the truck onto the bridge, at about the halfway point, my headlights picked up a large Goat that was standing in the middle, licking something off the surface. There must have been a shower of rain earlier because the surface was wet. The goat picked its head up and its eyes reflected back at us, there was no time to brake, besides, it was too dangerous. The lorry hit it, head on. There was a sickening loud thud and it was all over for the poor beast. Within thirty seconds, the big hard man from Glasgow was throwing up out of the window.

Another sad loss

Another job I remember doing was escorting a trainload of broken down military vehicles from Kuala Lumpur to the Royal Ordnance depot in Johor Baru. It took us all day to load the variety of vehicles onto the flat open railway trucks and chain them down. There were about twenty of us going with the train. We had been given plenty of compo rations and water for the estimated three-day journey. Most of the track was single line with passing places every forty miles or so. Our train was being held up every few hours on one of these passing places, while we waited for the very infrequent passenger or more important goods trains to go by. On the second day, as we waited, one of the lads spotted a small village about half a mile away through the bush. They put their dollars together and two volunteers ran off to find some beers. They were back in no time with several pint bottles of 'Tiger' one of the two brews available. The word quickly passed along the train and everyone was ready for the next suitable stop. It was amusing to watch as six Tommys raced across the undergrowth, their rifles across their backs, towards some little unsuspecting village and into the local shop to buy up probably their weeks supply of beer in one swoop. That evening, a group sat inside one of the ambulances on board, playing cards and drinking. The train rattled on throughout the night. We arrived at the big ordnance supply depot at Johor Baru the following afternoon and a roll call was taken, one of us was missing. Paddy Conner's body was found in two halves, a hundred miles back up the track. It seems he left the ambulance for a pee and fell between the open trucks, right across the line. His mate's thought he had gone to bed. I went to an inquest a week later and saw the photographs of his body, before, and after they stitched the two halves together, with what looked like very coarse string. It was a gruesome sight.

Back with the SAS

Some months later, I was attached once again to the same SAS outfit. The day I arrived, I drove up to the barrier at the camp entrance, jumped down from the truck and just as I was walking towards the Guardroom a bloody big python slithered between the gate sentry and me. It must have been ten to twelve feet long. As it slid past, I could see it was heading for a monsoon drain on our left. My instincts just kicked in, I dropped the documents I was carrying and grabbed the python with two hands around its tail. It had its head down a large monsoon drainpipe and was using the inside walls of the pipe to anchor its body. I was pulling like mad but couldn't get anywhere, it was gradually winning the battle and I had to let go. As I picked up my work ticket, I noticed an audience standing outside the guardroom watching me in amazement. The next few weeks were brilliant in that camp. Unwittingly they saw me as a bit of an expert on snakes and every couple of days, someone would come for a chat about snakes or bring me a dead one to identify. After a few beers in the NAAFI one night, one of the lads told me a story about a patrol he had been part of many months before, during the troubles. They had come across a group of terrorists and after a ten-minute firefight, only three CTs were still alive. The enemy dropped their weapons and stood with their arms raised in surrender. The patrol commander gave the order to fix bayonets and charge. During the charge, all three terrorists were killed by gunshot before the patrol reached them. He told me they couldn't take prisoners because they didn't have enough food or manpower resources to look after them for the ten-day march back to camp.

Tropical delights

I used to enjoy the fruits of Malaya, like the Rambutan and Langsat; these were passion fruits that were relished by the locals when they came into season. In addition, the much larger Mangosteen, which is also very delicious, but it took me a while to try the Durian fruit. This particular fruit had a terrible smell when it was opened; something like a cross between over-ripe cheese, rotten onions, turps and sewer drains, but it tasted absolutely gorgeous. If I became thirsty while driving, I would pull up in some little village and buy a piece of pineapple from a roadside stall. They would sculpture the Pineapple into wonderful spiral shapes, which got your mouth watering before you could get your money out. Other stalls sold ice slush mixed with fruit juice. Blocks of ice were kept in sawdust in a bucket to keep them frozen. The stallholder would take a brick size block of ice, wash off the sawdust and place it on a little hand operated machine that clamped the ice and spun it around over a blade. This sliced slivers of ice into a bowl underneath. These devices were no bigger than a hand operated sowing machine and could be found in every village and town throughout the country. Sometimes while waiting for my slush drink, I would be aware of some nearby Indian or Chinese temple, as my nostrils picked up the aroma of many burning Josh sticks. If it were a Chinese temple, the devotees would be burning imitation paper money, hoping to curry favour with their gods. Indian Temples had lots of candles and carved figures of people with elephant's heads and others with many arms. It was all very strange yet fascinating to me. I had grown to like these cultures and part of me wanted to stay here forever, among people I had become familiar with. However, memories of what I left behind were starting to take control. I spent more and more time thinking about my parents, siblings and friends back in Liverpool. The more I thought of them, the more I missed them and I found my parents appearing in my dreams but I couldn't see their faces. I started having vivid dreams again of flying over rooftops, high into the night sky. All I had to do was stretch my arms out in front and I would take off without any effort. My views downward were as real as if I was in a helicopter. I could see rooftops and roads as if it was real. I used to have these dreams often in my early teens. Sometimes I would be running along the pavement, taking longer and longer strides until my feet left the ground and I would skim along, twelve inches or so above the surface for miles.

Final days in Asia

It was a bit of a wrench but I had decided not to make a career out of the army. Three years was enough, I was missing my family, and home, so I wrote my letter of termination and a few days later was called into the office and listened to what my platoon commander had to say. "Driver Kelly, I have just the job for you. You will be the driver and personal escort to Major Dewhirst who is going to Borneo. He is an interpreter; your duty will be to take him to every little village in Borneo where he will liaise with the headman. This job is going to last for over a year. You are just the man for the job and you will be promoted to Corporal but it will mean signing on for a further three years."

He gave me twenty-four hours to make up my mind. I lay on my bed that night thinking it over and over, how would it affect me. It was certainly the kind of job I could go for, travelling all over Borneo, a different and bigger country, separated from Malaya by three hundred miles. What an adventure! However, on the other hand, could I enjoy travelling with an officer, being with him all day long, at his beck and call? I know what commissioned officers are like when things don't go their way. Nevertheless, he could be a really nice guy and I would be getting promotion to corporal, which means more money and status. Then again, there's no guarantee that all this would happen. I might sign on for another three years and they could turn around and say, 'Sorry, the job's been cancelled'. You could call this a crossroads in life, if I had said yes, where would I be today? I went into the office the following day to tell him I would not be signing on. The next three months were a torment, for the first six weeks, I was given all the best jobs; they were obviously trying to get me to change my mind and stay in the army. When they realised I was serious about leaving, I was thrown every bit of shit they could think of, but my mind was made up to think positive and get on with the job. The time actually flew by and very soon I was on a train heading south for Singapore docks.

Homeward Bound

My journey back home was interesting. It was on the troopship *'Empire Fowey'*, the same troopship that my brother Bryan had sailed to Hong Kong on in 1950. The Suez Canal had been re-opened, which meant that our journey would be two weeks shorter than the outward trip. When we arrived at Port Said it looked depressing, from what we could see; it was a filthy hovel as were the traders who flocked around our ship in their little dinghies, trying to sell hand carved elephants and other trinkets. A trader would throw a rope up to us with a basket on the end in which he placed an object hoping to sell. I pulled up the basket, took out the carved elephants I wanted and put in his money as payment. A commotion started further along the handrail when someone wasn't happy with his purchase and demanded his money back. The trader refused and all hell broke out when a fire hose was turned on and drenched the poor bloke in his little boat. Eventually, calm was restored when the perpetrator was arrested and sent to the Brig for a few days. Then another commotion kicked off when an Arab guy standing in his little boat decided to be a Flasher. He picked up his long shirt and wagged his old man up and down for all to see. This time, two fire hoses were turned on. The flasher made a quick retreat with his boat half full of water. A Pilot came aboard to steer the ship past the many sunken wrecks still littering the canal. It was strange to see so many funnels and masts sticking out of the water. I was surprised by the narrowness of the Suez Canal in some places. We were only yards from the banks where camel trains transported their goods. At the far end of the Mediterranean Sea, the ship anchored off Gibraltar where we had shore leave. Small ferryboats taking about three hundred at a time from ship to shore had us there in no time. My memories of Gibraltar were, cobbled streets, British Policemen, Red Post and Telephone boxes and Spanish bars.

Several hours later, I was on the last Liberty boat returning to the ship. We were still tied up to the quay and the Military Police were having difficulty trying to push the last thirty or so drunken soldiers, from the Welsh Guards, up the gangplank. Those already on board would not make way for them and were in boisterous mood. A lot of singing was going on with swaying to and fro and everyone else got caught up in the merriment. It was like a football crowd gone wild, the ferryboat was rocking so much that the gangplank became loose and crashed about twelve feet to the quayside with the thirty still on it. Nobody appeared to be injured and the MPs started blowing their whistles, drew their truncheons, and somehow got everyone on board. The boat was untied and started to move just as a last lone figure could be seen running through the dock gates. He was desperate not to miss the last boat home; the crowd on board was cheering him on as the MPs parted to give him room. His legs were flying as he ran down the cobbled surface and with an almighty leap, took off from the edge of the quay flying through the air across the widening gap; he missed and went completely under water. I happened to be the nearest one to his beret that floated up and managed to grab it. Two others grabbed his lapels as he broke surface and hoisted him over the rail like a drowned rat. He told us he had lost all sense of time while enjoying himself in one of the many brothels.

The ship docked at Southampton where the same train, 'The Borden Bullet' was waiting to take us back to the transit camp in Hampshire. There, we were processed for demob. We had a choice of being rigged out with a full suit of civilian clothes complete with hat, gloves and rolled up umbrella, if we wanted them. If so, we would have to stay another day and go to a different camp to be fitted out. None of us wanted to hang around any longer than necessary, sao we all chose to take the money offered instead, go home in uniform, and post it back to them.

Arriving Home

My train arrived at Lime Street Station, Liverpool at one thirty in the morning. I shared a taxi with a lad I met on the ship. His name was John Lennon and he was a brilliant Guitarist. However he was not the famous member of the Beatles. During the voyage, he would sit on deck in the evening and play to an audience of a couple of hundred men with his twelve-string guitar. We were all amazed by his mastery of the instrument, especially his renditions of fast and fiery Spanish music that often ended with a broken string or two.

The taxi dropped me off at Fielding Street and I was surprised how small it looked. It was either I had grown up or my eyes had been attuned to so much open space. I let myself in quietly with the key hanging on a piece of string through the letterbox. Everyone was fast asleep and stayed that way until I took Mam and Dad a cup of tea at six thirty.

Gerald, my second eldest brother, was still in the Royal Navy on aircraft carriers and was due for discharge in a couple of months after nine years service with the Fleet Air Arm. My big sister, Monica, was married and living near Low Hill with her husband Gordon. He was a taxi driver and they had two children. My eldest brother Bryan was married and living in Birmingham. Irene, my younger sister, was fifteen years old and still at school. Christopher the youngest brother was just twelve; Mam and Dad had high hopes for him. They had managed to enrol him in a better school, Cardinal Godfrey Roman Catholic High School. Dad was still working as a crane driver at Gladstone dock. My immediate thoughts as I passed him the cup of tea was, how much he had aged in just three years and yet he was still only fifty eight. The years of hard work and surviving two world wars had certainly taken their toll. Mother was fifty-two, still as slim and sprightly as ever, she was working in the Silver Blades Ice Rink in Kensington looking after the cafeteria. Her boss would often leave her to lock the place up. She said she was scared sometimes in fear that someone would be lurking in some dark corner of the building, especially when she turned all the lights out and had to find her way to the front entrance in the dark. Dad would often meet her there and walk her home. If Mam wasn't working at her job, she was either knitting or making soft toys for some friend's child. One of her favourites was a sitting rabbit with a large carrot in its hands. As Christmas approached there would be a whole variety of soft toys in the front parlour for people who had given her orders; it was one way of making a few extra shillings. My Nan who lived in the next street had passed away while I was serving in the Far East. I was very fond of her but they decided to keep her death from me for some reason until I got home.

My pal's brother was a serving member of the fire service and he did his best to get me to join Liverpool Fire Service but I had no stomach for it anymore. I had once loved being a fireman but through one moment of drunken stupidity, I threw it all away. It could have been a good life with a decent pension at the end but I knew my heart would never be in it. Another philosophy in life is, if you're not happy with your work, you should turn your life around and do something else.

Hackney Carriages

My brother-in-law got me a job on the taxis. I had to study the street guide for weeks and memorise as much as I could, then sit an exam and take another driving test before appearing in front of the Liverpool Watch Committee. I had to pay ten shillings deposit to Liverpool City Council for my lapel badge to be able to drive a black cab (I never did get my ten shillings back). It was an interesting job ferrying people from all walks of life to wherever they wanted to go. From tired mothers with bags of shopping on drizzly Saturday afternoons, spending more than they could afford on a taxi fare but desperate to get home to her waiting family, or the occasional wealthy celebrity who thought nothing of putting a five pound tip in my hand for a three hundred yard journey from the Empire Theatre to the Adelphi Hotel. Then chatting to those who wished to be chatted to and leaving others to themselves, who were lost in their own little world, and the seagoing ships' Captains who lived across the water in the Wirral and were greeted by their lonely wives outside their beautiful houses with well-kept gardens. On the other hand, the prostitute who needed help rectifying some minor problem with her front door lock before heading off for an evening of trade.

Then there was the Barclays bank manager who was cutting costs by hiring my cab instead of an armoured car to transport a million pounds to another branch in the city. Four bank staff in suits carried an enormous holdall across the pavement and into the cab. Three of them were carrying truncheons and one actually sat on the bag of money as I drove off. Every day or night was different; it was a satisfying and rewarding job, which was not without its hazards. Dealing with drunks, washing vomit out of the back of the cab before plying for further hire;

getting fleeced by a gang of lads late at night, when they ran off without paying the fare. Being pulled off a rank by the Hackney Carriage Police because your taxi isn't deemed clean enough. I got a call over the radio one night to pick up a fare at the Ninety Social Club in Everton. It was one thirty in the morning when I pulled up at the side entrance and knocked on the door. 'Come in' someone shouted, I pushed open the door and stepped in to the pitch-black entrance. 'In here' the voice called out again as I fumbled my way in feeling for the next door handle and pushed my way into the main clubroom which was also very dark. 'HAPPY BIRTHDAY PETE' a multitude of voices cried out as all the lights went on. I was taken aback as my brother-in-law, big Mac and about fifteen other cab drivers as well as a crowd of regular customers had given me a big surprise. We spent the next three hours celebrating my twenty-third birthday and someone dropped me off home in the early hours of the morning. My head was in a bit of a mess when I was awakened at ten-o- clock by a banging on the front door. 'Where's the cab Pete?' It was the day man who had come to pick up the taxi. It took me a few minutes to get my brain into focus and started recalling where and what had happened the previous night. Finally, it came to me that I must have left it outside the Ninety Social Club. The day man had been brought to the house by another mate in his cab so we bundled ourselves in and drove up to Everton. When we went around the corner into the alleyway where the side entrance was, there was the cab safe and sound but the engine was still running and had been ticking over for the last nine hours. It's a wonder nobody hadn't noticed and reported it to the police. A vehicle left running nowadays with nobody in attendance would probably disappear within as many minutes. The Liverpool taxis were equipped with a fantastic anti-theft device, which raised the wheels off the ground. Each wheel had its own hydraulic lifting jack attached to the axle and could be operated by hand from under the bonnet, thus eliminating the need to struggle underneath, especially in bad weather, to change a flat tyre. I was caught out one night, I called in over the radio to Mersey Cabs, 'Charlie Two, can you get someone to come and tow me in, I think the half shaft has broken'. The reply came back, 'Charlie Two, make sure your rear wheels are on the ground, over'. Without answering, I sat there for a few moments pondering the last instruction then finally leaving the driving seat to have a look at the wheels. Sure enough, they were two inches off the ground, and then it dawned on me that one of the other cabbies had jacked me up during the thirty-minute lull before closing time at the Chalk Farm public house.

Thick as a Pea Soup

Over a period of about five days in December 1952, four thousand people died in London from the effects of smog. This was called the Great London Smog and it initiated the Clean Air Act. We also had terrible smogs in Liverpool; the last one I remember was in 1962. I walked home from work one evening with one hand holding a wet handkerchief over my mouth and nose and the other hand stretched out in front of me. The smog was so thick; an arm's length was the limit of my vision. All traffic had come to a standstill; double deck buses were parked in side streets for the night. There was an eerie quietness about the place; the smog was even damping down noise. The air was full of nitrogen oxides, carbon monoxide, sulphur dioxides and who knows what volatile organic compounds. It tasted awful. I bumped into an old couple going the opposite way, 'Where's Edinburgh Road son?' the old man asked. 'I think you've come past it,' I replied, but I wasn't sure. It was impossible to see street names and you had to have a good memory for corners of buildings to keep your bearings. Eventually, I got home and looked in the mirror. Two streaks of yellow and black soot marks went down each side of my nose, disappearing up my nostrils. This was the pollution in the air. A terrible murder had happened that night in Old Swan. A young woman answered her front door and a knife was plunged into her body. I'm not sure if the assailant was ever found but it was a shock to the whole of Liverpool and something that frightened a lot of women. How our world has changed in such a short time. As I write this story in the year 2008, murders seem to be happening almost every day. Nevertheless, Home Office figures say that violent crime has dropped considerably of late.

First White Wedding

Very soon, I met a young lady who turned my head; we seemed to hit it off from the word go and started courting seriously. I was introduced to Else on a blind date that one of my mates had set up. She had beautiful long auburn hair with natural waves. Unlike most girls, she never wore make-up and her skin was pure and fresh. Within two years, we had saved up enough for a proper white wedding. Else was Church of England but she wanted to be married in my Church so she took some lessons in my faith to satisfy the church authorities and we went ahead. We married in the second week of September 1961. It was a beautiful sunny day; this was the first white wedding in both our families. We were surprised how many people apart from guests had turned up at the Church. My Dad, always the joker told Else that he'd paid them all half a crown each to come.

The reception was held in the rooms above the Gregsons Well Inn, West Derby Road. My cousin, Tony Frost was in the Police Force and he arranged a sextet live band to play for us. They were all members of the Liverpool Police Band.

We had a wonderful evening and retired happily to our wedding bed where we consummated our betrothal for the first time. I have always been very proud and full of admiration for my young virgin wife in persuading me to wait for that very special moment.

I had invited my cousins from Yorkshire, they had moved there from Liverpool during the war when their house in Parliament Street was bombed. One of them offered us a room for a week and the following morning we drove to Yorkshire and spent our honeymoon in a cottage in the village of Luddenden.

We had a glorious week discovering the area and fell in love with the place and it was then that we fostered an idea of living in Yorkshire. My opinion was that if we were going to have children, then I would rather they were brought up surrounded by fields, farm animals and fresh air and give them a better start in life than mine.

Billy's Lost Teeth

One of my brothers-in-law, Billy Taylor, lost his upper denture one night after a heavy drinking session. As a merchant seaman, he'd had the denture made in the Far East; it was an elaborate affair made of platinum and gold. It had cost him quite a lot in Far Eastern terms but worked out very much cheaper than having the same thing done in the UK. Billy turned the house upside down, searching frantically for the elusive item and wasn't looking forward to the date he had fixed up with his new found lady friend that same evening without his denture in place. It was only a small plate which consisted of one front tooth and another one at the side which he had decided to have made in gold. It gave him a look of class so he thought when he walked out of the dentist's office in Bangkok. Several months later, his ship was back in Liverpool after another World Tour for the rich and famous, and Billy walked down the gangplank sporting a brand new denture just like the old one he'd lost. He was determined this time to take more care when out drinking. He had managed to get a twenty per cent reduction from the dentist by feeding him a cock and bull story about them coming loose while leaning over the ship's rail. On arriving home after every voyage, the first thing Billy did was to take his mother out for a meal. It had become a ritual ever since he first went to sea as a young boy of sixteen. Billy was now in his middle forties and Mum was the most important woman in his life, even though she was now in her late seventies. He had phoned Mum from the ship to tell her to get ready. She was upstairs when his taxi brought him home. He asked the driver to hang on a couple of minutes while he bounded up the stairs two at a time. 'Ready Mum?' She was dressed in her black heavy coat with the astrakhan collar, a little leather handbag and black leather gloves gave her a look of elegance. 'Mum, you look radiant in that outfit and who gave you that beautiful brooch?' He leaned forward to get a better look. 'My God' cried Billy, under his breath, 'Its my teeth'. His Mum who was short of hearing and would only use her spectacles to read the births, marriages and deaths in the Echo replied, 'There must be something wrong with the clasp son, I had to fasten it to my coat with a safety pin'.

Yorkshire Tales

A year later we moved to Luddenden and took a rented cottage for ten shillings a week. All our furniture which was on the never, was brought up to Yorkshire on the back of an open coal lorry and tied on with washing lines. I led the way along the East Lancashire road in the 1949 Ford Anglia we had bought second hand for forty-five pounds. I drove a couple of times around most roundabouts on the journey waiting for the little old lorry to catch up. It would never have climbed up over the high moors so I led him the longer way through the valley via Todmorden and Hebden Bridge. As soon as we had the furniture indoors, I left Else to sort out the bits and pieces while I went looking for a job. I started work the following morning as a machine minder in a local factory making nuts and bolts. The noise of one machine nearby, a cold header, made so much noise, my head was aching. There were no such things as ear defenders so I only stayed two weeks in that place. Most of the people working there had been there years; they were nearly all deaf and had mastered the art of lip reading. I got to know a chap who lived near us who was employed as an inspector in a large engineering firm in the valley. He told me about a vacancy in his department for another inspector. I had no experience whatsoever in engineering but was formulating a plan to try and secure that job for myself. Over a few pints, I gathered as much information out of him as I could, in what skills were needed. Two days later, I was sitting in the manager's office telling him I'd been working for a company in Liverpool for several years and had to move to Yorkshire because it had folded and there was no work in Liverpool. I'm not one for telling lies but this was necessary for my future. I gave the name of the only firm I knew in Liverpool who had gone bankrupt; it was a shipping office where my brother-in-law had worked as a clerk since he left school, Marwood and Dowey. The manager at the engineering firm and I seemed to get on well, the interview was going great and my accent must have convinced him because he gave me the job. I knew he couldn't ring up anyone in Liverpool to ask for my credentials. On Monday morning, I was in a brown smock, checking the work of skilled men with micrometers and slip gauges. Somehow, I bluffed my way through the first day and soon settled down to a quite well paid job. The following spring, I started getting itchy feet for the open road, this job had been ok during the winter and I enjoyed my work but I couldn't see myself being stuck indoors all through the summer. I heard a whisper that a firm up the valley was looking for night drivers. Two weeks later, I was behind the wheel of a new BMC van with environmentally controlled air conditioning, delivering day old chicks to holding units all over the north of England. Thornbers was one if not the biggest producer of egg laying birds in the country and they had chicken farms all over the place. Farmers loved their hybrid hens that could lay eggs faster than any other, which meant bigger profits for the egg producers.

The day old chicks were a product of hybrid parent stock from local farms. Fertile eggs were collected daily and brought to the hatcheries at Mytholmroyd, where they spent twenty one days being gently heated and turned in automatic incubators. Hatching was co-ordinated to four days a week, Monday to Thursday. On these days, there was a flurry of activity in the hatchery as thousands of chicks were separated from their discarded shells and sent to the sexing department. There they had their bowels emptied by one of the sexers who pointed the chick's bottom towards a small bowl while giving them a quick squeeze of the abdomen before examining their private parts. Hens were thrown down one shoot while the young cockerels were thrown down another. At the bottom of the shoots, they landed onto a conveyor belt where they travelled along in separate channels. A team of women picked up the females and packed them into boxes of one hundred, while the unwanted cockerels were left to complete the journey to the end of the belt, where they unceremoniously fell off, into a large dustbin. All the time, they would be chirping away, with no idea of their sex or fate. The females would start their journey in our vans, to a life of egg laying, never coming into contact with the opposite sex. A few years later, when their usefulness of producing eggs was finished, their bodies would end up on the menu of some cheap eating-house or fried chicken outlet. The males started their short lives by struggling to get to the top of the dustbin, only to find their world suddenly thrown into darkness, and taking their last breath of air before the lid was put in place and the gas tap turned on. The young lifeless cockerels had one more journey to make. Their remains were picked up by tractor and trailer in the late afternoon and taken to a farm run by another company at Wadsworth in Hebden Bridge. They were put into a big mincing machine and the slop produced was fed to the many caged and ferocious Mink animals that were being bred for the fur trade. This farm became the target of the animal liberation front one night, when they broke in and released hundreds of Minks into the countryside. Others condemned their action when the ferocious mink roamed the land and decimated the wildlife in the area. I am glad to say there is no trace of the farm anymore. On the site now, stands a crescent of beautiful homes. Our boss, Cyril Thornber had big ideas in the poultry world. I was one of four night drivers whose job was to arrive at the hatchery at four thirty in the afternoon. We loaded up the specially built vans with the boxes of chicks and prepared ourselves for the journey. The new born hatchlings had to be delivered throughout the night to 'Holding Units', these like the vans, were environmentally controlled with fans for warm weather and heaters for the winter. The firm's farm reps, who had taken the orders, would pick up the boxes of chicks with their smaller vans the following morning and deliver them to their customers, some of whom were in very remote corners of the countryside. We, the 'Bulk' drivers would drive up to four hundred miles a night over a period of fourteen hours. There was no such thing as Tachographs in the cabs to measure the hours driven, the Ministry of Transport had not got round to it yet. I enjoyed driving through the night, as there was very little traffic on the roads, although the journeys could sometimes be quite boring.

I secured a battery operated portable wireless in my cab on a shelf above the windscreen and would listen while driving to stories by Valentine Dial (The Man in Black) or Thirty Minute Theatre from nine to nine thirty pm. The BBC would close down at midnight so I would tune into Radio Caroline and other illegal offshore radio stations and listen to the early years of Tony Blackburn and others broadcasting pop music. Sometimes if there weren't many chicks to be delivered, two of us would double up by putting both loads onto one van. It meant more miles but it gave us the opportunity to have a rest with two drivers.

One winter's night, on just such a long journey near Mount Snowdon in Wales, the van broke down on the A55 outside the little village of Llanberis. We found a telephone box and rang our mechanic in Mytholmroyd, West Yorkshire who was at home but on standby. I reckoned it would take him three to four hours to get to us and it was freezing cold with no engine to provide the heating. We gathered some fallen wood from a nearby copse and lit a fire near the van, we didn't want the chicks to freeze to death and we were also feeling the bitter night's temperature. After a while, the fire gave out too much heat and we feared it would start blistering the paint on the van so we had to push the vehicle a bit further along. Then, we couldn't find any more wood to burn and finished up standing in the back with the chicks for warmth. To pass the time, we played noughts and crosses on the cardboard boxes. What seemed like an eternity later, the mechanic arrived and replaced a cracked injector pipe from the diesel pump. The engine was ticking over in no time and as we were clearing away the last embers of the fire, we watched the mechanics taillights disappearing towards Shrewsbury. I started to drive off in the opposite direction but within a hundred yards, the engine spluttered and died, the early diesel engines were notorious for air locking. The mechanic had not bled the system thoroughly enough, and we were back to square one. Mobile phones had not been invented and there was no way of contacting the mechanic until he arrived back at his home base. It was now four thirty am, only two vehicles had passed in the last four hours and a third was just coming into view. It was a brand new chassis and cab that was being delivered somewhere; we got the driver to give us a tow. It took seven miles of towing at about twenty-five to thirty miles an hour with my engine in third gear before the airlock finally cleared and the engine burst into life. I blasted the horn to signal to the towing driver. After unhitching ourselves, we got under way. We were so relieved to feel the heat coming back into our bones once more and continued the job of delivering our load of livestock to the unit near Holyhead, Anglesey. It was almost midday when we got back to the depot in Mytholmroyd.

Thornber's had a small team of scientists who were always experimenting with one thing and another and one day, they arranged for a small light aircraft to drop a box of day-old chicks by parachute onto the land behind the hatchery. Their idea was to create a faster delivery time to isolated farms in northern England and the highlands of Scotland. The chicks survived the parachute drop with no adverse affects but the idea was dropped after an anonymous phone call was made to the local RSPCA. We in the transport department couldn't believe that someone would get so uptight about giving a few birds that don't normally fly a wonderful freefall experience.

The firm decided to go into the sheep breeding business. Their scientists reckoned they could get a lamb to have two pregnancies a year by keeping them in controlled environment conditions. In other words, have them in sheds where the lights would go off and on every eight hours or so, to kid the sheep into thinking they were living two years in every one thus giving birth twice when we all know that lambing happens only once a year. They bought some very special sheep from somewhere abroad and were arriving at a quarantine unit at some railway sidings in central London. The animals would have to be looked after for the length of time they were in quarantine and it was my job to take one of our shepherds down there, complete with a caravan for him to live in. We got there and set up his mobile home then waited for the arrival of his new stock. A few hours later, a train arrived with the eight very special and expensive sheep. These we had to transfer into pens within a big shed purposely built for keeping animals. The shepherd got inside the train carriage and passed them over the top of the half door one at a time. I grabbed each one by their thick wool and placed them into the pens. I received a scratch on my cheek as one of them was kicking quite a lot. Some weeks later, the scratch turned bad and I had to have an operation to remove a lump that had developed on my cheekbone. It cleared up fine afterwards and all I was left with, was a small round scar. The cost of buying these sheep, transportation, having a shepherd to look after them for three or six months (I never found out which) must have been enormous. I had been given a large lorry to drive delivering sectionalised poultry houses to farms all over the country. This was another department of the massive firm; they manufactured and erected the poultry buildings wherever the customer was. At that time, I wanted to educate myself further and bought some books entitled, teach yourself Maths and English etc. Sitting in my cab one day and thoroughly absorbed in my learning; I became aware of someone looking over my shoulder. The loading team was watching me through my cab window and soon after, I had the nickname of 'Professor'. This actually gave me encouragement and spurred me on to continue studying. I did well at my own pace over the next few years and became quite competent. I particularly enjoyed helping the kids with their homework, little did they know, it was helping me also. But as time went on, Susan in particular was learning stuff that was way over the top of my head and the only way I could help her

155

with her homework when she got stuck with maths was to ask her to retrace to the point where she did know. It worked every time, suddenly she would say, 'It's ok dad, I know where I am now'.

First Motorcycle

I once saw a film of men riding big motorcycles across America with the wind blowing through their hair, and I had dreams of doing the same. My ambition only got as far as buying a second hand Matchless 350cc for twelve pounds ten shillings in the early 1960s. Up to that point, I had very little experience of motorbikes and somehow managed to persuade the thing to keep upright and stay on the road. After a few days, the insurance company sent a man around to take my certificate away; he repaid my money saying they had made a mistake in letting me have insurance in the first place because I was only a provisional licence holder. The maximum capacity was 250cc and my bike was deemed to be too big for a learner rider. I couldn't let a little thing like this spoil my dream, I just had to make sure I became a safer rider; after all, I needed it, to get to work. Fate took control of my illegal mode of transport a few days later on Saturday afternoon, when the clutch decided to stop working. I sat down at the side of the road with my little tool roll and took the clutch cover plate off to investigate. Ten minutes later, I had a pile of clutch plates, thrust plates, rods and springs etc., by my side and had to admit defeat. Fortunately, I had broken down right outside a pub in Horton Street, where I went in to phone Cable Motors, a motorcycle dealer in Halifax. Thirty minutes later, a pick-up truck arrived to take my bike away for repair. That was the last I saw of that machine. The cost of repairs had been far more than I paid for it, so I left it with them. I still had the old logbook up to a few years ago and the registration number would have brought me a lot of money, if I had been aware of its value. People pay good money for a cherished numberplate to sport on their car. I just forgot all about the logbook and left it lying in a drawer until it was too late. A year later, I bought a Honda 250, which was far more reliable and trustworthy. I gained a lot more experience and booked myself in for a driving test. It was 2nd January, the weather was awful and my examiner had his umbrella up as he watched me doing circuits of the Town Hall in Halifax. He said, "Keep going around the block, I am going to step out between some parked vehicles and I want you to carry out an emergency but safe stop while keeping the machine under control". Cars and vans were parked all around my route so it could be anywhere that he decided to jump out. However, I was ready for him and made a perfectly executed emergency stop. He seemed quite impressed but he didn't realise that I had seen the tip of his umbrella over the roof of the Transit Van he was hiding behind. After that, it was just a matter of answering a few questions on the Highway Code and receiving the all-important piece of paper showing that I was now a competent rider of motorcycles. As I am now over seventy years of age and having owned more than a dozen motorbikes of all sizes over the years, I consider myself very fortunate for never having had an accident. My philosophy on these machines is, you never stop learning. I still have one today and enjoy the thrill every time I take it out.

Back among the Commies

In 1963, I drove a large lorry for my firm, to an International Agricultural Exhibition in Yugoslavia. The twelve hundred-mile journey would be quite normal today for heavy goods vehicles, but in those days, the roads across parts of Austria and most of Yugoslavia were nothing more than farm tracks.

The open deck lorry with its high load got almost stuck under a bridge in Salzburg. It was Saturday morning and the Autobahn by-pass had been closed for the weekend and was being used for motorcycle racing. I was trying to find a route through the town centre and came to a low bridge, approaching very slowly, with my upper body hanging out of the open door, trying to watch the overhead electric trolley bus cables. Just as I was deciding the load wouldn't go under, I heard a loud police siren behind me. A not so friendly policeman beckoned me back away from the low bridge and gave me no help whatsoever with an alternative detour. He got back in his car and disappeared, leaving me to struggle through the narrow streets. Later that day, I arrived at the border crossing between Austria and Yugoslavia. I asked the customs official, how often do English trucks cross this border. The official had been a prisoner of war in Cumbria England. In faltering English replied, "The last British truck that went across this checkpoint into communist Yugoslavia three months ago was never seen again", and he drew his fingers across his throat. I did notice a twinkle in his eye.

The customs inspector gave the load a cursory glance but was more interested in the 'Plumb' well that's what it sounded like. The plumb turned out to be the lead seal that had been applied to the ends of a long piece of string that had been laced through the eyeholes of the wagon sheet and the body hooks when I docked in Belgium. The ends of the string were brought together and tied in a knot and a lead seal squeezed onto the knot with an official looking Customs impress.

If he had shone his torch along the string in either direction, he would have seen several other knots that didn't have seals. This was because, on entering Austria several days before, I had to remove all the ropes and sheets at the side of the road to reposition the load, which had started slipping.

They opened the barrier and I drove along the unlit road for several hundred yards and came to a scene that could have come out of a James Bond film. The border Guard dressed in a drab looking green uniform with an automatic weapon slung over one shoulder was standing near a red and white painted oil drum. A striped barrier pole barred my way. To one side of the road was a collection of small wooden buildings. On the other side was a forest of tall pine trees. Unlike the country I had just left, this one was dull and threatening looking. Streetlights were few, the lights in the buildings looked dim, thus casting eerie looking shadows around the place. The Guard examined my papers and indicated that I must leave my lorry on the no-mans land, side of the border until the next morning but I could cross and use the facilities available. I was served a coffee in the small café by a young woman who had no interest in her job and with a face that could have come from any funeral cortege. I didn't want to chance my luck by asking her for the menu and retired to my truck where I broke open a new packet of biscuits before getting my head down for the night. I didn't hear one vehicle pass through the checkpoint before dropping off to sleep an hour later. The following morning brought me to the now open freight office, my papers were scrutinised and I was asked to pay thirty three thousand Dinars to use their roads. A large sign on the wall read, "All Foreign Currency must be exchanged into Dinars". As I was carrying about nine hundred of the firm's pounds, I took a chance and kept my mouth shut and changed just two hundred. It was a good job I did because three weeks later, coming out of the country, was another sign reading "Maximum amount of Dinars for exchange 5000 any excess will be confiscated". My firm would have lost a lot of money if I had followed the rules and I would have had no money left for fuel. On my way into Yugoslavia, the roads in were atrocious; I was down to twenty miles an hour over the rough surface, strewn with potholes. The Lorry was lurching badly. After a few miles I could see another big lorry coming up fast in my rear-view mirror, he overtook me doing about sixty and disappeared in a cloud of dust. Over the next thirty minutes several other wagons came past, all doing the same speed, I noticed how steady their loads were, so I decided to increase my own speed. Once past fifty miles an hour, the truck and load kept as steady as if it was a tarmac road. The wheels and springs were taking all the shock and it was pretty noisy. I arrived at the town of Novi Sad at seven pm and found the place I needed. The next morning I unloaded the lorry with the help of two labourers supplied by the authorities of the show ground. At nine o'clock, a customs officer in uniform and with a pistol hanging off his belt came to examine the goods coming off the truck. The load consisted of a sectional poultry house that had been designed for such events. When assembled, the rectangle timber building had one wall and gable end missing to let people see inside. There were also several crates containing battery cages with automatic cleaning devices, electric motors, show stand furniture, several chest freezers and a full size gas spit and barbecue. There were also many other items such as literature and notice boards, all packed in wooden crates. As each box was opened, the customs man peered in to make sure that everything was above board and listed on the carnet and I was not bringing any contraband into the country. The carnet or manifest was written in four languages, English, Belgium, German, and Yugoslav for the convenience of all customs officials on route.

An hour later, he told us to stop work and indicated to me to follow him to his office. Inside, he beckoned me towards a couple of comfortable lounge chairs; he called something in his language towards a curtain hanging over a doorway at the back of the room. He could speak hardly a word of English and I was even worse with Serb or Croat or whatever he was uttering but somehow, we understood each other. I was made to understand that it was a day of celebration, being the first day of May. Marshal Tito was the leader of this communist country and I was to learn over the next few weeks that the majority of people liked him very much. His was the giant photograph I'd seen so many times since crossing the border into Yugoslavia. The curtain opened and a woman with long black curls and dressed in some sort of traditional costume, reminding me of an old fashioned Gypsy, came in with a tray of small cups, glasses and a very colourful and ornate metal jug with a long handle and spout. She poured out some brown liquid into the tiny cups while he filled the glasses with some kind of wine. Being the perfect host, he waited for me to start, I didn't know which to drink first, and I opted for what I now knew was black coffee. There was no milk or sugar on the tray and they were very small cups so I had no difficulty in downing the contents in almost a mouthful. It was extremely strong, thick and gritty and hit the back of my throat with a vengeance. Trying not to show distaste, I decided to wash it down with the wine, which turned out to be Slivavica, a very potent and strong tasting Yugoslavian brandy made from plums.

My throat was now on fire and I politely refused a top up.

Jim, a joiner from our firm and Harry a salesman, arrived by car and caravan. Over the next five days the three of us had the stand erected. We built the battery cages and had the electric motors wired up to the mains. The power supply had no neutral; a single strand of live current was all that was supplied. To get the machines working, an earthing wire was connected up to the framework of cages and tied to a steel rod, which was thrust, into the ground. Anyone touching the metalwork could feel a slight tingling sensation. This was very unorthodox and the safety people in Britain would have been appalled. Our firm was sharing the stand and cost with two other companies who were in the same line of business. Cobbs Broiler Chickens and Meat Rabbits and Bernard Matthew's Turkeys. All three firms were showing live stock and the day before the opening of the show, I took the lorry to Belgrade Airport to pick up the several crates of live birds and rabbits and a few crates of dressed frozen birds that had been flown out from England.

After ten days, the exhibition came to an end and the upper echelons flew home. It was left to Jim and I to pull the stand down, repack, and load the lorry. We were instructed to slaughter all the livestock and dump them. This was to make sure the protected bloodline of the animals didn't fall into competitor's hands. The local poor people who hung around the showground looking for whatever they could find, thought it was their birthday when we gave them freshly killed turkeys chickens and rabbits. Whether the show was a success, I don't know but I enjoyed the five-week trip to this communist country and came home with some good money, most of it being won from the three company directors when we played cards.

It was the night before our last night and my boss Terry, a director of the firm, decided to give his other two colleagues a bit of a do in the caravan. They had been staying at a hotel in the town for the last ten days. I cooked several frozen chickens in the oven of the caravan and we all had a decent meal washed down with plenty of wine and beer. Somehow, we started playing cards with the Dinar money and when all that was gone (into my pocket) they started playing with sterling. We were playing Three-Card Brag, a game I learned in the army and was quite good at. By the end of the night, I had won over a hundred pounds; my wage in 1963 was eighteen pounds a week. Bernard Matthews, the millionaire, asked me to lend him twenty pounds for his taxi fare from London Airport to his place in Norwich. (I got it back later.) This has always been my claim to fame.

On my return journey I had to pay another fee of 36,000 Dinars at the same checkpoint, for using their roads once more (about

£35). This gave me a good chance to get rid of the surplus Dinars I had in my pocket, as their currency was worthless and not recognised outside their country. We made it back to the docks in Tilbury where the customs men wanted to examine the load. OK I said, where do you want to start. I'll undo the ropes and you can do the rest. It was an enormous load, covered by three tarpaulin sheets and tied down with several long haulier's ropes.

After a half-hearted attempt, they told me to be on my way, "Thank Christ for that" I thought, driving through the dock gates, they never spotted my smuggled hoard.

Downhill without Brakes

Back in England, they gave me the job of taking loads to all the agriculture shows from one end of the country to the other. I was driving down Pool Bank in Yorkshire on my way to the Great Yorkshire Show at Harrogate with a nine-ton load when the brakes failed. A set of traffic lights was on red and I couldn't stop. The brake pedal was pushed to the floor and with one hand on the horn and the other desperately pulling the handbrake, there was no response. I was approaching the junction at about thirty miles an hour. The first car to appear from my left, luckily was being driven by an old man and he was slow getting off the mark, if it had been a whiz kid, he would probably be dead now. I shot past and missed his front bumper by an inch. Several cars coming uphill towards me were flashing their headlights; I couldn't stop and careered down the hill. The lorry I was driving had ten forward gears and two for reverse. I was in third gear and the engine was screaming like hell and was gathering speed. I switched the ignition off, pulled out the engine stop, the engine was now retarding, and lots of black smoke was coming out of the exhaust. It seemed to be doing the trick, but the power steering wasn't working without the engine and I had to work hard with only one hand on the wheel and the other on the handbrake. Having just got round a long left-hand bend, the road started levelling out. Luckily, the second sets of lights at the bottom of the hill were showing green, I shot through them and the road started levelling off, I was able to come to a stop about two hundred yards on.

'Phew! That was a close thing,' I said to myself, then went to find a phonebox.

I enjoyed working for the firm and was able to see the length and breadth of the country and some of Europe. My journeys took me to many farms over the years, in some remote and beautiful settings, particularly in the highlands of Scotland where I was once given a big fresh Salmon that one of the farmhands had tickled out of a local stream. However, I was spending too much time away from home. My wife was missing me, and my children were losing their Dad's identity; I was missing so much of their growing up period, it was time for change.

Back in Uniform

It was some years earlier that I became a member of the Yorkshire Volunteers. I was still doing my army reserve and decided that joining a local outfit would be better than going down to Hampshire for two weeks every year. The trouble was that I soon became involved with the TA and spent more time away from home than I planned.

In no time, I was promoted to Corporal and in charge of an infantry section. We carried out lots of training and honed our shooting skills to a very high level. Our shooting team became legendary within the battalion and won more trophies than any other in the north of England. The following year saw us down at The National Shooting Centre, Bisley in Hampshire, where shooters from all over the world went to compete. Our team came back with a suitcase full of trophies. Like the others in our team, my mantelpiece at home was getting pretty crowded. The following year, the whole battalion moved to West Germany for two weeks where we took part in a massive NATO exercise to show the Eastern Block a bit of muscle. I went with the advance party by road to Hull where we drove all our vehicles onto the *Sir Gerraint*, an LSL (Landing Ship Logistic). We landed at Zeebruger in Belgium and convoyed eastwards where we joined up with many thousands of other troops, tanks and planes from lots of NATO countries, making, one long line of forces stretching all the way down the border of the East German Republic. We carried out our bit of the Chess Game for two weeks and returned home. No doubt the Generals were patting themselves on the back at having shown the Russians what we were made of but we did have four fatalities from the Parachute Regiment when they accidentally dropped by parachute into a wide canal with all their equipment on.

In 1972, I was promoted to Sergeant, the army pay was going a long way to keeping the family in good stead, but it also meant more time away from home. The following year, I self discharged and settled down to family life and started enjoying the last few years of my kid's lives before they grew to a point where they would begin feeling grown up and wanting to fledge their own wings. My energy and spare time went into gardening, I grew all our own vegetables and salads. I would come home from work and after tea, would disappear into my garden until it went dark.

Camping Capers

Every year I would plan the summer holiday for my elder brother's family and mine. We couldn't afford anything more luxurious than a week under canvas, but those holidays were always far more enjoyable than some I've been on in recent years. "We want to get an early start," one of us would say, after arranging to meet somewhere along the route. Therefore, at some ridiculous hour in the night, we would set off to beat the traffic jams. Bryan travelling from the Midlands and myself from Yorkshire would aim to rendezvous at about the halfway point. Else and the kids would get their heads down in the back of the old van and try to catch up on their sleep while I concentrated on the route. Climbing up the mountain out of Llangollen, I came across a large hand-written sign on a piece of cardboard at the side of the road, it read, 'Hurry up Pete'. I recognised my crackpot brother's writing. Bryan was one of those characters in life who worked hard all year and put so much effort into his free time by letting all his inhibitions go out of the window, and was determined to enjoy his holiday from the word go.

Five minutes later, I came across two figures walking towards me in the early morning mist along the A494; it was Bryan and his young son Grant. They had broken down and were walking down the mountain to find a telephone box; these were still the days before mobile phones. Within an hour, his car and camping trailer were being winched up onto a low loader with the compliments of his AA membership.

He was able to pick his car up a few days later from a local garage in Porthmadog, North Wales, where a new half shaft had been fitted. All of us in the meantime, had started our holidaying big in style by creating a family commune out of our two large frame tents and uprighted camping trailers at the council run campsite on the beach. Later in the day, another small and distant family group arrived from Scotland as scheduled, the commune grew a little more and we all had a brilliant summer holiday. This type of annual migration went on for several more years until the children decided they were too old to go with their parents anymore. Without kids in our company, it wasn't the same. We had no excuse to run around being daft or playing games on the beach or chasing rabbits and seagulls just for the hell of it. Our holidays became very tame with visits to museums, country houses, churches and pubs. I in particular missed my kids coming on holiday but they were starting to feel grown up and would have had the Mickey taken out of them if they had told their friends they'd been on holiday again with their parents.

An Opportunity

When I was a kid, I had an insatiable curiosity about what made things work. My mother told me in later years that I would take all my toys apart, including my sister's dolls to see how their arms and legs were kept on. I couldn't put them back together again which got me into trouble more than once. I was just curious which resulted in me getting an electric shock by sticking my fingers in the light socket, but this didn't deter me. Now I was grown up, an opportunity to fulfil my enquiring mind came to me one day, when I saw an advert in the local paper. The advert read: W*anted, a good all round man who has experience in engineering, machine repairs, electrical work, welding, etc., and is in possession of a heavy goods licence.* The only requirement I possessed was the Heavy Goods Licence but this didn't stop me from being ambitious. I had learned the rudiments of welding at Thornbers when I pestered one of the lads in the workshop to show me. I turned up for the interview wearing my army pullover and the boss's son who was only fifteen, was mad on anything military. When he found that I was a serving soldier, his mind was made up. It didn't take much persuasion for him to convince his dad that I was the man for the job. They were a small firm who refurbished bakery machinery and catering equipment. I was in my element with all these machines to strip down, rebuild, and more importantly, finding out how things worked. One day, my aspirations went a bit too far when a small complicated food processor I had stripped down resulted in a bench full of mysterious looking pieces. I couldn't get the thing back together, there were some parts left over, and I gave it up as a bad job and put the whole lot into the scrap bin without the boss knowing. The whole place was full of all sorts of second hand machinery, so the one I had just binned wouldn't be missed. My self-esteem was renewed later in the day when one of the lads owned up and admitted, as a joke, he had added some extra parts to the pile on the bench while my back was turned.

When pieces of equipment left our premises, they looked like brand new with shiny new paintwork and re-chromed metal handles etc. I was made Foreman after a couple of months, only because they took a few more people on. There was one particular make of machinery that was more complicated than others. The Hobart range, one of their own engineers would come in doing 'Foreigners' in the evenings and weekends, earning extra money to supplement his income. I could never get to watch him doing his work, as he would stop whenever I approached, thus keeping his skills and the mysteries of the Hobart machines secret. After about a year, the boss told me that 'Bill' the Hobart man was coming to work for us full time. I couldn't understand why he was leaving a good job like that to come here but maybe the boss made him an offer he couldn't refuse. We heard later that he wanted to stay local instead of driving all over Yorkshire. The following morning, Saturday, the kids and I were going to the swimming baths. Walking past the job centre, I noticed Bill's old job being advertised in the window. On Monday morning, I phoned the job centre for an interview and ended up getting the job. I became a mobile service engineer, with a vehicle provided, a good salary and expense account and apart from courses, was home every night. The Hobart Corporation was American owned, with a massive factory in Ohio, USA. Their European headquarters were in Offenburg, West Germany, where I was to visit four times for two weeks at a time over the next five years on technical courses, learning all the secrets of how they were put together. Some manufacturers build their products so they can't be repaired by the man in the street. Sitting there during my third course, I couldn't believe my luck, or was it determination that brought me from being a Pawnbrokers lad to a highly trained technician. I just loved learning and soaking up knowledge. On returning to England, I was summoned into the office and given a letter that had come from the training school in Germany which read, *'Peter Kelly has shown exceptional aptitude and concentration to his course and has passed the examination with high marks. He will be an asset to his employers'*. My first thoughts were 'someone's taking the piss'. I don't ever remember bringing a school report home, probably because I was so thick, they didn't want to waste their paper.

Enrolled at Liverpool University!

My brother still left me to organise the summer holiday and one year I came across a holiday with a difference. Several Universities were opening themselves up to people who enrolled themselves on various courses of interest during the summer recess. Instead of laying off the admin staff during the half term break and having to hire them again for the next term, the authorities in charge decided to bring in paying guests throughout these quiet periods. I sent for a leaflet and put the idea forward. Our wives thought it would be over their heads and didn't fancy the idea of going back to school, even if it was only for a week. However, they did want us to go; I think they were looking forward to some time to themselves. I filled in the application forms and was looking forward to learning all about stained glass windows and how to make them. The course was being held in a beautiful old converted corn mill on the edge of a river in the county of Suffolk. Unfortunately, when the applications came back, the stained glass window course was fully booked and our second choice had been allocated. Neither of us had any idea what Transactional Analysis was, but thought, 'What the hell we'll give it a try'. The main reason I opted for this course as our second choice, was its location. It was at a Liverpool University College in Chester, that beautiful old walled city on the river Dee. We arrived at the old college and were shown our rooms, which were not much bigger than a Monks Cell, or what I imagine a Monks Cell to be. The room had a single bed, a bedside cabinet and wardrobe. A writing desk with shelves that almost reached the ceiling, this would be for the many books that University students possess. The window overlooked a large garden and grounds where the sounds of birds filled the air. The communal toilets and bathrooms were down the hallway. An hour after enrolment we assembled in the large hall where we arranged chairs into a big circle. I think there were about twenty-five men and women in the group. The tutor, a lady who was heavily pregnant and very confident looking, addressed us and asked us to state our name, occupation, area of residence and the reason why we were here. She pointed to the person on my left to start. Listening to each person speaking, I felt slightly exhilarated at being in the company of so many educated and distinguished people. There were several academics and schoolteachers, two Neuro-Surgeons and a Royal Naval Commander retired, among other professions. One person said, "I am here because I have studied Freud's theory of personality and systematic psychotherapy for personal growth and change and I would like to take it a stage further". I thought 'What the bloody hell is all this about?' I had to admire the tutor who stopped us at the halfway mark and reaffirmed everyone's name from memory. I said to myself, 'Wow, I'd like a memory like that'. We carried on until it was my turn. I just happened to be the last one. Taking a deep breath and mustering all the confidence I could, said, "My name is Peter Kelly, I am a self employed catering equipment engineer, I live in West Yorkshire and I am only here because the stain glass window course was full". There was an outburst of laughter from everyone present, the ice had certainly broken and the atmosphere changed within a second from apprehensive to relaxed. After a few days, we started to understand what it was all about and enjoyed the experience of learning a new concept. Bryan and I especially enjoyed our visits to the Olde World pubs in Chester in the evenings, where we could start mimicking one or two posh talking members of the group. Jeffrey for instance, the RN Commander had a deep slow voice. He told us earlier that he had been brought up in a strictly controlled family atmosphere where his father had told him many times to 'Grow up' and 'Don't act childish' just when he should have been a child, enjoying all the things that growing kids get up to. Jeffrey was now in his fifties and had the bearings and mannerisms of a stuffy old man. He couldn't easily laugh or take part in light-hearted banter. He thought the world of us two and said he felt relaxed in our company because we acted the goat when not in lessons or we were just plain silly with our repartee. So it became obvious why this man had come on the course, he was trying to find and recapture the child ego within himself. We learned that everyone has three ego states, the parent 'Exterpsychic' state in which people behave, feel and think towards others, as would a parent towards children. Then there is the Adult 'Neopsychic' state, which some people favour over others. And the Child 'Archaepsychic' state, where people can be creative, feel free and have little concern of what others think of them. In this state, they can also throw tantrums if things don't go their way; you will know people who are like this. However, we all need three ego states and variations of them to live happy and contented lives. This explanation is just a very small example of the theory of personality. I found it extremely interesting and have benefited from its teachings over many years. On the final day of the course, the tutor seemed to be psychoanalysing various people within the group, giving them therapy and helping them with their hang-ups. She addressed Bryan and myself quietly, saying, "There's no need for you two to take part in this" On the last day of the course, we each had to write our names on a piece of A4 paper. They were all placed on a table and each student took someone else's paper, made a personal comment about them and fold it over before taking another. At the end of the exercise, each of us would make a written comment about every other person on the course.

We were instructed to take our own paper and read what others had said about us.

Unfolding my paper and reading what other people thought about me left me in tears.

Prior to that moment, I had no idea how people saw me and to become aware of your own idiosyncrasies and attributes from a close group of others has an amazing effect on your being. The love and warmth that was written down in all those separate comments gave me goosebumps and it took some time to get over the experience.

'*Did time stand still?*'

We had a family gathering at our cottage in Yorkshire, after spending the evening in the village pub, where we had been celebrating my fiftieth birthday. The drinks were still flowing and our satellite-scattered families were making the most of being in each other's company, by catching up with family gossip and past memories. It was near two in the morning when I said to Else, my wife; "I am just going to take the dog for a final walk for the night". We walked down past the Lord Nelson Inn, the last remaining village pub, dating back to 1634. This is the Inn where Bramwell Bronte, Emily Bronte's brother used to stop for a drink in the 1840s on his way home. Emily was the famous author of 'Wuthering Heights'. Bramwell was a clerk at Luddendenfoot Railway Station and he travelled on horseback from Haworth every day. Ben, our black Labrador was as lively as ever, sniffing here, cocking a leg there as we crossed the deserted high street and entered the 'Ginnel' (an old Yorkshire word for passage or narrow path). Down to our right lay Saint Mary's Church, where I suddenly heard the faint sounds of approaching footsteps. I was curious as to who else was out and about at such an early hour. Looking over the chest high, dry stone wall, I focused my eyes and ears towards the footsteps on paving slabs. I recognised the sound of the steps; being made by footwear that had long gone out of everyday use. They were clogs, not modern white clogs that are often used by Chefs in kitchensm, nor fashion clogs worn by trendsetters, but iron shod clogs that were worn by Mill workers in the eighteenth and nineteenth centuries. The last time I had seen this type of footwear being used was nearly forty years before, by an old man who lived locally. He became a bit of an attraction when he was out and about, and the unfamiliar sounds of his footwear were the first thing people noticed.

It is thought that clog dancing originated in the Mills when men used to dance to keep their feet warm and amuse themselves from boredom by clicking their clogs to the rhythm of the looms. I stood, staring at the path less than fifty yards away but could see no one. The footsteps were still coming towards the church entrance. The front entrance was well illuminated by an outside light over the door but I could still see nobody approaching. My thoughts were centred on the amount of alcohol I'd taken during the evening and soon dismissed the idea of being over inebriated because I have never been a regular big drinker and this party was no exception. I blinked my eyes to get a clearer view, the path was empty. Turning my head slightly, to make sure Ben had not run off, I was amazed to see him standing perfectly still, facing away from me. He was not moving a muscle; this was not like him. Just then, the footsteps stopped right outside the front door and before I could take another breath, the church bells struck two o'clock. The sudden sound startled me and I stood transfixed, staring at the non-existent person who had walked up to the entrance. The church did not have a porch where anyone could hide so where was he or she? I waited a good ten or fifteen minutes to see if the wearer of the clogs, having somehow deluded my sight, had been relieving themselves in the shadows and would continue on their way. Nevertheless, not one more sound came from that area. I decided to leave and turned around to see Ben, still standing in the same pose, like a statue. "Ben" I called and had to repeat, "Ben", a little louder, before he snapped out of whatever trance he was in and returned to his usual scurrying and leg raising. We returned to the cottage where most people had retired to bed. "Where have you been all this time?" my wife asked. I looked at the clock on the mantelpiece, it was three thirty. I had to check several timepieces and was mystified at being out for over an hour and a half, I could swear it was no more than fifteen minutes.

I do not believe in ghosts, the hereafter, or so-called spirits, except those that come out of a bottle. I have a logical mind, if a thing can't be understood, then it needs more investigation. I can understand and accept some of life's mysteries, like magnetism, electrical current and black holes in space. They are all feasible but for the life of me, where is the sense in saying we have a spirit that survives after we die when there has never been one shred of proof other than from people's own imaginations? I did tell my family about my experience the following morning then dismissed it as a figment of my own imagination. I would love to come face to face with a ghost, I can't imagine being scared but I would be very curious.

Back in Bandit Country

Like most people, I had a curiosity about my roots and started a tentative search for my ancestors. The first step in any genealogy research is to prove who you are. A look at your birth certificate will show yourself, your parents and your father's occupation. The next step is getting hold of your parents and grandparents birth, marriage and if appropriate, death certificates. Before long, two of my brothers and I were diving headlong into our own family history, which took us into the archive sections of various libraries in Lancashire. We spent hours trawling through microfilms and microfiches, ending the days with stiff bottoms and raw eyeballs, sometimes going along the wrong route and being frustrated by it all. After a while, we decided to go over to the Irish Republic to try and find where our Grandfather was born. The only information we had, was a written document from our own father before he died, telling us his family came from Blackrock, Dundalk. Bryan and I took the Car Ferry from Liverpool to Belfast, arriving on a Saturday evening and found a hotel on the edge of the city. After a good night's sleep and breakfast, we paid the bill and walked out into the car park. Both our mouths dropped open, last night, the car park was full, in fact we got the last available empty space but now, ours was the only car there, it looked very strange out there in the middle, all on its own and we wondered why? This was Northern Ireland, which was going through the troubles; the IRA was constantly at loggerheads with the British Army. Shootings were happening almost every night and in fact, we had heard what sounded like a gunshot in the early hours of the morning. Over the past ten or so years, shopping centres and public buildings had been blown up and many people had lost their lives. Then why did we go you might ask? Because the troubles had been going on so long, people on the mainland had become immune to the stories about Northern Ireland. It was old hat and had become a boring subject. Anyway, this trip was exciting and as we had both been soldiers, it brought back a bit of nostalgia. As we walked towards my car, I sensed something wrong, where was my brother? I looked around, he was still in the doorway of the hotel, "I'll let you start the engine Pete" he shouted. 'Bastard' I muttered under my breath while I was laying down on the car park, searching for any wires that showed a bomb had been fixed under the chassis. Why would anyone want to booby trap my car, you might ask. Because it had English number plates and, it was the only car left outside the hotel. When Bryan got in the car he said, 'There was a big Disco last night that's why the car park was full'.

Within minutes, we were driving through the city, past several burnt out cars and buses. Armoured vehicles, manned by British troops stood on street corners. Members of the local fire service were coiling up their hoses and police were standing around looking tired, it had been a normal Saturday night in Belfast.

Our research was across the border in the Republic and we were soon heading that way along a spanking new road with hardly another vehicle in sight. Eventually, we crossed the unmanned border into the Republic and immediately noticed the difference, the road surface had become uneven, bumpy and in need of repair. After a mile, the road signs showed we were back in Northern Ireland then another few miles we were heading for the border again. "This is crazy", one of us said. The border in this area twisted around so much that a straight-line route causes this effect. The locals call this area, 'Bandit Country', not without reason. We passed a sign at the side of the road, which read, 'Welcome to Derry, We Aim to Please', underneath the words was the black silhouette of a rifleman laying down and aiming his weapon. We came to a large army checkpoint, all vehicles passing through were being stopped and searched. When our turn came, a young soldier from the Anglian Regiment approached and asked me a few questions and checked my driving licence, which has to be carried in NI. While this was going on, his colleagues were training their weapons directly at us from their prone positions in the hedgerow. 'I hope those lads have had good training and know which way the safety catch is' I said. Bryan replied, 'They wouldn't have live ammunition in their guns would they?' 'Get yourself on' I replied in a strong Northern Ireland accent, 'They certainly won't be blanks'.

A mile or so across the border we forgot all about the troubles, the countryside rolled out in front of us like pages from a tourist brochure. The Irish Republic is a wonderful place to visit; the people are so friendly and accommodating. Later that day, I pulled up to a classy farmhouse, making enquiries as to where we could pitch a tent for the night? After a knock on the door, the lady of the house invited me in; her husband was sitting at a large kitchen table drinking tea. 'Will you take a cup?' she asked as he beckoned me to a chair. Bryan had decided to stay in the car. There was no enquiry from either of them as to who I was or why I was there. We chatted for a while about the weather and where I lived in the UK, then eventually I was able to ask him about pitching a tent. 'Have you seen anywhere you would like?' he replied then went on to say, 'I wouldn't put your tent in the bottom field, the cows being nosy will probably wake you up in the morning'. The Irish landowners are so generous in these matters and would never consider turning anyone off their land as long as they are behaving themselves and cause no damage. A few days later, we were having a pint in a nice country pub where we met three men from Lancashire. They came to spend a week every year fishing on the numerous lochs and lakes between Sligo and Athlone. There are reputed to be three hundred and sixty five places to dangle your worm in, the same amount as days in the year. The Irish landowners actively encourage fishermen to come on their land and fish to their hearts content at no charge. The year before we arrived, the Irish Government introduced a fishing licence. These three guys each bought a licence but found they were not allowed to fish anymore at their favourite spots. The farmers and landowners eventually got the licence scrapped and status quo reigned once more.

Our research hit a blank wall after talking to many people and searching several graveyards then realising that Kelly is the second most common name in Ireland. Most of their public records which were stored in Dublin, had been destroyed in a big fire in the 1940s.

Back home, we decided to trace our mother's line, which is of Scottish descent and discovered that our grandfather was born illegitimately in Wrexham, North Wales. His grandfather came from Loth in the Highlands of Scotland in 1860. He was a Tea Merchant in both Loth and Wrexham and it is possible that he sailed from Loth to Chester on a tea Clipper around that time.

Head above the clouds

My enquiring mind kicked in once again and I was keen to find the answer to a question that had been bugging me for years. How does a great lump of metal in the shape of an aeroplane defy the laws of gravity? I started taking flying lessons at a small flying school on the edge of Leeds and Bradford Airport. It was a brilliant but rather expensive hobby. However, as I had never smoked in my life I considered that this was much cheaper than cigarettes over the years.

To fly a small two-seated plane was one of the most exhilarating pursuits I had encountered so far. I had an introductory flight during which I took over the controls after we got airborne; this was exhilarating and spurred me on to take proper lessons. The following week after a short time in the classroom where I had it explained to me about curvatures of wings and speeds of air over them that creates lift, the first flying lesson saw me taking the plane off the ground. I couldn't believe that I was sitting on the runway of a commercial international airport, waiting for the invisible vortexes of a holiday jet that had just taken off in front of us, to dissipate. The turbulence of a vortex could flip a small two seater aircraft upside down.

During my second lesson, my instructor wanted to show me the 'effects of controls', in other words, what happens to the aircraft when different levers and pedals are pushed and pulled. He eased the stick backwards and we climbed up to four thousand feet where he pushed it the opposite way. The aircraft's nose went down, we started dropping towards the ground like a stone. I felt as though I was on some giant fairground ride. My eyeballs seemed to be popping out of their sockets as the aircraft screamed towards the earth. Through my earphones, his calm voice was saying, "You will notice as we descend, the speed indicator is increasing and the altimeter is decreasing". All I could see was the dual carriageway between Keighley and Skipton coming up towards me extremely fast. The cars that had been pinpricks way back up there at four thousand feet were now rapidly growing in size. He pulled the lever back at about two thousand feet and the plane came out of its dive. "I want you to take over control and repeat the same manoeuvre", he said. I was very busy, swallowing hard and trying to keep back my breakfast which had reached my epiglottis. Somehow, I managed to hold onto the contents of my stomach and complete the same climb, dive and pullout. After landing, I got into my car to drive home but only managed two hundred yards before pulling up and letting it all go out of the open door. The third lesson, the following week, saw me landing the plane, which was another exhilarating experience. I had to approach the airport at two thousand feet and line up with the runway from a long way off. I couldn't see it at first amid the fields and houses. When it did come into my view, it looked like a tiny strip of tarmac no wider than a suburban street. I had to align the aircraft up and approach at the correct angle of descent. This was achieved with the help of some lights at the beginning of the runway. Too high or too low and the lights showed the wrong sequence. Two white lights and two red lights indicated to all approaching pilots that you were in the correct angle of descent and you were not going to land too early in the rough, or overshoot the runway at the far end. I felt quite confident that everything was going well and carried out all the instructions coming through my headset from my flight instructor. Coming in to land at seventy miles an hour can be a bit hairy, particularly when a fresh breeze is blowing across. A gentle push on the left rudder kept the plane straight; a light backward pressure on the control lever and the Cessna made a beautiful feathered landing. A few weeks later, I graduated onto a new aircraft, the French built Avions Robin, carried on taking lessons for a few more months, up to the point of flying a circuit of solo, and then called it a day. I reasoned that if I got my flying licence, what would it do for me? I couldn't buy myself an aircraft and I was too old to become a commercial pilot but I had satisfied my curiosity and thoroughly enjoyed the journey along the way. What's more, the question, 'How does a big lump of metal defy the laws of gravity' had been answered.

Wonderful Europe

We were touring through southern Spain in 2002 when I caught a bug that put me in hospital for three weeks. It was a viral infection called Streptococcus and it knocked the hell out of me. We had no idea where it came from, after many questions from the doctors; they were as mystified as I was. The Spanish hospital doctors and nurses did a wonderful job in getting me back to good health and I thank them for the care and attention I was given. While I lay recovering, I thought how fortunate we Europeans are in this twenty-first century. Not long ago, we were all fighting and killing each other and now we have freedom to move and work anywhere we want to throughout the continent. We can get assistance at the drop of a hat and through the mobile phone can be in touch with our family and friends within seconds. My doctor in the hospital would only discharge me providing I didn't drive the twelve hundred miles back to the UK. We took a plane and within the next few days, I was having my liver scanned in our local hospital at Halifax where they found no trace of the killer bug, just a couple of scars, where a colony had been.

The specialist there was very pleased with the treatment I had been given in Spain and remarked, "You wouldn't have got that treatment here on the NHS". I was glad I was in possession of my

E111, the European medical card which gives you full medical cover in any emergency throughout Europe. I must also give praise to my insurance company 'Direct Line'. They sent a man out to Spain to pick my car up. I had made arrangements to leave the caravan there for the following year. They brought my car back, had it valeted and delivered to my front door and it didn't cost me one extra penny. We have grown to love Spain and its people; they have a wonderful way of life. They are very family orientated; they love their children and old folk alike. There are very few old people's homes in Spain because the families stick together and look after each other. They love their celebrations and every city, town and small village will put so much effort into their festivals and Saint's days. Spain is currently suffering from an influx of undesirables from other countries within the EU and some countries outside Europe. Some of these people have no desire to work other than breaking into isolated properties and robbing whatever they can carry. Unfortunately, a few residents of these types of houses have suffered at the hands of these thieves. When people sell up in Britain and move to other countries, they sometimes view the world through rose tinted glasses and everything looks wonderful. That beautiful villa in the countryside is just what they've been looking for. Unfortunately, it's just what the thieves have been looking for also. The next thing that happens is, more money has to be spent on security, high fences and gates with intercoms and finally, guard dogs that bark all night and annoy others. A dog's bark can be heard from a long way off in the middle of the night depriving people of a good night's sleep. Those nice people have now become neighbours from hell and nobody wants to know them, they have become prisoners in their own homes. After a couple of years when all the excitement has worn off, they are fed up of having nobody to talk to and the house is put on the market, a market that has fallen so much in the last few years. I have seen this happen so many times and I feel sorry for those who have been persuaded to purchase by some smooth talking estate agent. It's not my place here to tell people what to do and where to buy, I am just pointing out a few facts that may help the prospective purchaser in foreign countries.

El Burro's Dinner

It was a beautiful sunny day in Andalucia. I took my motorcycle for a spin around the local countryside. I use tarmac roads only to get me to an area where I can go off road along the myriad of dirt roads in Spain. I really should have bought a dual-purpose bike that was more suitable for this terrain but I seem to have mastered my heavy 250cc-road bike over the rough tracks. After a couple of miles or I should be saying kilometres now, I came across a teenage boy pushing his bicycle towards me. He looked hot and tired as I approached and I got the feeling that he was in some sort of trouble. "Esta usted bien?" I asked as I pulled up. "Mi bicicleta esta quebrada" he replied. I had asked, "Are you alright?" He replied, "My bicycle is broken"

Author and Wife in Spain

and showed me where the frame had snapped cleanly in half. Then assuming I was as good as he in speaking Spanish, he rattled on like a machine gun. I caught one word in ten and got the gist of what he was saying. He had been out collecting food for his Burro and couldn't get it back to his parent's house on a broken bicycle. I told him to get on the motorbike behind me and within minutes we had gone another mile along the track to where he'd abandoned his load. I thought, 'no wonder his bicycle snapped if he carries such weight over the rough tracks'. He lifted up the enormous bundle of fresh green fodder and plonked it onto the pillion seat behind me. The load pushed me forward onto the petrol tank. He then leapt up on top of the bundle sitting high above me as we set off towards his home. "Cual es su nombre?" he shouted, "Peter" I replied, "What's yours?" "Fernando, y muchas gracias". My only regret is not having a photograph, which would have taken first prize in the agrarian section of some likely magazine. We arrived at his village amid stares from several passers by and stopped at a ramshackle house where his father was sitting under a tree in the shade.

I was introduced to 'Padre, Madre, Hijos and Hijas' (father, mother, brothers and sisters). It was a good opportunity to practise my faltering Spanish. By the time I left, to the sound of many thanks from the whole family, I got the feeling they all seemed to enjoy my being there. On my way home, I thought, 'There is a family, struggling to make ends meet. The fifteen-year-old son goes several miles away to collect food for their only means of transport, the donkey. Moreover, how people complain in Britain when their benefits Giro cheque is a day late in coming'. These Spaniards, all had smiles on their faces, they were poor, but they looked happy and contented and as far as I know, they receive very little in benefits compared to us.

Conclusion

As I am writing, I can hear fireworks going off in the distance, it is Easter Sunday and the people of Spain are celebrating as ever. We now live in the beautiful country of Spain full time, and we are both in our seventies. I'm doing my best to learn the Spanish language, I paint and keep fit with daily mountain walks. Else loves living here, she also walks and pursues her passion for cooking which delights my stomach. We both have far more friends than we ever had back in Yorkshire and we are two very healthy and happy people.

I just want to tell you a story about the kind of people, the Spanish are. Several years ago when I first arrived here, I bought myself a second hand bicycle in order to join the Monday cycling group. Approximately ten or twelve neighbours would meet at eleven o'clock every Monday and cycle to nearby villages and towns where we would take a Tapas lunch, then come back via a different route through the orange groves and farmland. We were all pensioners so the pace was quite gentle which suited everyone taking part. I needed a couple of new tyres, especially one for the back wheel, which was only just holding in the air. Someone told me about a shop in the town of Garrucha. The following weekend, we took the car to do the weekly shopping there and find the bike shop. The lady in 'La Bici' amazed me when I decided to buy two new tyres, but on looking in my wallet, only had the price of one. I put my ten Euro note on the counter and indicated that I was sorry but only had enough with me for just one tyre. She pushed both tyres toward me plus the ten Euro note saying "Venga adentro manana y pagueme" (Come in tomorrow and pay me). I couldn't believe the trust she was showing me, a complete stranger. This was not an isolated case either as I have been treated similarly on several occasions over the following years by various Spanish people.

Now before you all think I've gone completely soft and turned my back on the place where I was born and brought up, let me tell you where my true feelings lie. I have been fortunate enough to travel the length and breadth of Great Britain, meeting and talking with and listening to almost every dialect spoken. I have travelled a fair

Peter

bit around the world, have met many cultures and lived among a few, and there is one dialect that is instantly recognisable to my ear wherever I have been. One group of people who will readily communicate with each other no matter which part of the planet they are in. They could be among a large crowd of mixed races on a beach in Singapore, waiting in a queue outside a theatre in London or fishing on a river in some quiet backwater in Australia. It doesn't matter where they are, Liverpudlians will meet and greet each other like long lost relatives. What I have noticed is the immediate bond between strangers who share this same culture and I am very proud to belong to that group of warm-hearted people.

The End